# "SHE IS EVIL!"

## MADNESS and MURDER in MEMPHIS

### JUDITH A. YATES

**WILDBLUE**
PRESS

WildBluePress.com

*Some names and identifying details have been changed to protect the privacy of individuals.*

SHE IS EVIL *published by:*
WILDBLUE PRESS
P.O. Box 102440
Denver, Colorado 80250

*WILDBLUE PRESS is registered at the U.S. Patent and Trademark Offices.*
ISBN 978-1-942266-26-6    *Trade Paperback*
ISBN 978-1-942266-98-3    *eBook*

*Interior Formatting/Book Cover Design by Elijah Toten*
*www.totencreative.com*

# DEDICATION

For all of the women and men who find themselves victims of domestic violence, I hope and wish that you may find peace and escape safely.

Thank you to my family, who taught me respect and kindness, for myself as well as for others.

Tina Marsh, you are an original. Tell your stories, my friend.

… And especially for …

Ejaz Ahmad: *Assalamu'alaikum wa rahmatullah wabarokatuh - May the peace, mercy, and blessings of Allah be with you.*

- Judith A. Yates

# AUTHOR'S NOTE

"She is Evil!" is not a fictionalized version of the murder of Ejaz Ahmad. The narrative is based on thousands of hours over several years of interviewing, researching, and reviewing documentation including reports, legal transcripts, photographs, media, court reports, and numerous other resources. All persons mentioned are real, but some names have been changed to protect privacy. Although a work of nonfiction, the nature of the story necessitated the need to recreate some conversations, which was done based on extensive research, because no verbatim record exists. These alterations are as minuscule as possible in order to remain authentic to the story. Some people refused to be, or could not be, involved in this project; therefore, their involvement in the story stems from the recollection of events of other sources. This information was researched and evaluated by the people involved and me in order to be as accurate as possible.

Our hope is that, as a result, if even one person can be saved from a violent, deadly relationship, if even one victim can be assisted in escaping domestic violence, Ejaz did not die in vain.

# PREFACE

This book is not about any particular practice of faith being "right" or "wrong," good or bad. It is about domestic abuse spiraling out of control, and about how other factors, such as mind-altering substances like drugs and alcohol, along with unchecked or unbridled anger, and weapons can destructively conspire together to create chaos. And about how all of this can lead to an individual winding up in a cellblock ... or in a graveyard.

For over twenty-five years, I have been a domestic violence prevention educator. My own family was touched by this evil. After the incident, I found myself consumed with anger. I had to harness that anger, not facing it meant sitting in a prison of emotions, so I educated myself. I went to college, and attended classes, lectures, and workshops, and using the information I learned, I began to teach others. Once upon a time, my family did not believe domestic violence could touch us. I strive to explain to all families that it can, and it is so simple to fall into it, as both a victim and as a perpetrator, if you do not know the warning signs, or if you do not understand the cycles of violence, and if you have no outlet or safety net, or have been isolated from them.

In an effort to understand the key players in this story, I found myself studying Islam, the Muslim faith, and the culture of Pakistan. Like any holy text, portions of the Quran can be taken out of context. Faith is an interesting concept; the study of where we place faith and its traditions is fascinating.

"Muslim" is not synonymous with "terrorist." To compare all Muslims to a few fanatics is akin to comparing all blonde-haired, blue-eyed American white males to Timothy McVeigh (who was executed for his role in the 1995 Oklahoma City bombing of the A.P. Murrah Federal Building). There are fanatics in all faiths who use religion to justify their evil deeds. The United States and Pakistan both have histories of violence. Violence exists in all holy texts because violence always has been, and still is, unfortunately, a part of life.

I hope this book serves to provide the reader with a new understanding about crimes involving domestic abuse, and the evil that can surface, causing people to do heinous things to one another.

-Judith A. Yates

# CHAPTER 1

*In time of distress a man can distinguish
between his friend and enemy.
Iman Ali (circa 1650 A.D.)*

By now April was over, and ten-year-old Jordan Ahmad was antsy. He had not heard from his father in three weeks, and he missed talking to him. Jordan and his father, Ejaz Ahmad, shared a close bond. Jordan had called his father's house, but the only person who would answer was his father's new wife, Leah. "He's not here," she would answer when Jordan asked. Sometimes she would say, "He's in West Memphis right now." Finally, she told him that Ejaz had gone to visit his home country of Pakistan, but even as a young boy, Jordan knew that did not make sense.

Jordan's mother, Bonnie Garrett, was divorced from his dad for the second and final time, but she and her family still loved Ejaz. Ejaz and Bonnie respected one another and had remained friends. Ernestine Marsh, Bonnie's mother, adored her grandson, and still loved Ejaz like a son. She would overhear Jordan on the phone, asking for his father. He always waited and then hung up, dejected.

Ernestine discovered Leah had told Jordan his father was in West Memphis, a small town just over the bridge west of Memphis, Tennessee. She also discovered that Leah had a different response each time Jordan called.

Bonnie had made her own calls. Bonnie told Ernestine she had also spoken with Leah, and about how Leah was giving strange answers as to Ejaz's whereabouts. Bonnie, along with her brother, had gone to Ejaz and Leah's Memphis home and knocked on the door, but no one had answered. She had even gone to the mosque where Ejaz worshipped, but they told her the same thing, "He has not been here for weeks."

Ernestine decided it was time for some answers, as she had decided that Leah was not forthcoming. It was so unlike Ejaz to not call or visit with his son, was and it would have been totally out of character for Ejaz to go to Pakistan without telling anyone. Ernestine knew her ex son-in-law was not an impetuous man; he consistently considered his family first and foremost and reliably kept them apprised of his travels. Ejaz was neither selfish nor mean, and he had a good soul, but Ernestine had heard some rumblings about Leah.

On May 1, 2003, Ernestine and Jordan headed for the home his father shared with his new bride, Leah Joy Ward Ahmad. Ernestine parked her car and the two went to the front door to knock. "It looks like Leah's moved!" Ernestine exclaimed. Gone were the numerous cars Ejaz owned. There was junk on the carport. The front yard was mowed, like Ejaz liked it.

"Let's see if his stuff is still in there," Jordan told her. They had to go to a side window, located under the carport, to cup their hands around their eyes and peer in. "All his stuff from his store is gone!" Jordan said, a strange sound in his voice.

"We have to go," his grandmother told him. "I want to speak to the neighbors."

As they rounded the corner to walk towards her car, Ernestine heard some children across the street. "They've moved!" the kids shouted, indicating Ejaz's home.

Ernestine walked across the street to ask the kids if their parents were home. When their parents stepped out on the porch, Ernestine introduced herself and Jordan.

"Oh, the woman over there had a big moving truck the day before. She had the cars hauled off the next day," a neighbor told Ernestine, pointing at Ejaz's home. "She told me her husband was in Pakistan, and she was selling the house 'cause she couldn't afford it. I haven't seen the man there in, oh, probably three weeks or so."

"He's not in Pakistan."

"Oh. I don't know." The woman bit her lower lip, then volunteered, "They been havin' parties over there. She has a man come over and mow the lawn."

"I'm going to give you my number," Ernestine reached for her purse. "Will you give me yours?" They exchanged phone numbers, the woman promising Ernestine she would call her if she saw anyone at Ejaz's home.

After speaking with the neighbor, Ernestine and Jordan were returning to the vehicle when a little neighborhood girl, trying to help, told them, "There's a chicken still in their yard."

"That's my chicken!" Jordan exclaimed. He had kept a pet hen in his father's backyard, and he told his grandmother that he wanted to get the hen and bring it home, explaining his concern that it would starve if no one were there to tend to it.

"Do you have a cage to put it in?" Ernestine asked.

"Yes, ma'am!" He took off running towards the house, glancing up at the storm clouds gathering in the sky.

Ernestine walked towards the unassuming ranch style home, frowning at the trash on the porch and tightly drawn shades. She followed her grandson around the side of the carport to the back of the house. She was taken aback by the junk strewn on the back porch and in the yard: a workout station, boxes, and debris. The back yard was overgrown. This was so unlike Ejaz!

She looked over at Jordan who was dragging a cage around to the front of the 9' x 10' metal tool shed that was in the yard, and then began chasing after the speckled hen.

Ernestine let herself into the back yard as the hen dodged into the tool shed; the bird was forced to squeeze in between boards that were propped up against the shed's open doorway.

"Eew!" Jordan had stopped short of chasing the hen into the shed so that he could pinch his nostrils to try and block out the offensive odor. "I smell something!" "Yeah, but it's not your chicken," Ernestine said, nearly gagging as she walked over to join him.

Jordan studied the small metal shed where his pet had her nest. His father stored various items in the shed. The doors were missing, and the boards which his chicken had managed to squeeze through were blocking the entryway. One by one, he removed the boards, placing them aside. Inside the shed and to the right, a motorcycle and several car doors were neatly stacked against the inside wall. An outdated cash register sat on a back shelf among tin cans and car parts. To the left was an old eggshell foam mattress cover that looked out of place. Flies buzzed about, rising in small clouds from the mattress cover.

"It *does* smell bad." Ernestine, with her hand covering her nose and mouth, stepped forward next to Jordan. Nose wrinkling at the stench, he asked his grandmother to lift the foam to peer underneath, which she did.

Ernestine stumbled backward out of the shed, trying to catch her breath. She nearly fell over Jordan. Jordan panicked at what he saw. Both stared in horror at the shed. In her heart, Ernestine knew at that moment what had happened to Ejaz.

Soon, police sirens were wailing through the quiet suburban neighborhood.

# CHAPTER 2

*Allah will not change the condition of the people*
*until they change what is in themselves.*
*- Sura Ar Rad 13:11*

Pakistan is a beautifully rugged country despite the unrest lying deep below its geographical surface.

The world's sixth most populous nation lies on the collision point between the Asian and Indian tectonic plates, massive slabs of solid rock that developed early in earth's history; drifting very slowly and tapping one another as if to remind the earth it would be always be moving, shifting.

Pakistan rests between China, to the north, and India to the south and east; Afghanistan is northwest, with Iran to the west. There is a long-standing disagreement between Pakistan and India as to which country claims the mountains of Kashmir and Jammu. Thus, even geography plays a part in the tremulous existence.

Further contributing to this are the shifting cycles of weather. Spring and summer tend to be hot and dry, with temperatures reaching to a hundred and ten degrees (Fahrenheit) or more. Monsoon season lasts from June to September. December through February brings a notable drop in temperature.

Political unrest and upheaval have tampered with the economic potential of Pakistan, where textiles, labor, and rice are exported and petroleum, machinery, and steel are imported, along with "black gold" – oil. Up to fifty percent of the country lives below the poverty line. Like any social dilemma, there is no one cause for this high poverty level. To contribute to their family's finances, children work in the mines, in tobacco fields, and in other precarious places of employment, including brothels. It is a dangerous cycle:

lack of education leads to low wages, a legacy passed down through generations.

An unsteady history, as jarring as the tectonic plates underneath, plays a role in the problems faced by Pakistan. Although the nation is fairly new, huge cities have existed there for at least five thousand years. Once there were grand civilizations, large urban centers, created by the Indus Valley people who would eventually mix with Aryans. As a result, the Vedic Culture was established, along with the birth of Hinduism.

After the reign of Alexander the Great, Persians and then Greeks exerted an influence over Pakistan.

In the eighth century A.D., Muslim traders not only introduced goods and services to the region, but also their religious beliefs. Islam became the state religion between 997-1187 A.D.

A succession of changing leadership followed: Turk/Afghan through 1526, Babur (a descendent of Genghis Khan) until 1857, and the British until 1947.

After World War II, Muslims from British India objected to uniting with the nation of India. The parties agreed to the Partition of India: Hindus and Sikhs would inhabit India; Muslims moved to Pakistan, the new nation.

Today Pakistan's fragile federal government works to balance in a democracy. The ceremonial figurehead, the President, has the constitutional power to pass bills and declare ordinances. The Prime Minister is the chief executive and has the responsibility of running the government. There is a two-house system of parliament of a one hundred member Senate and a three hundred forty-two member National Assembly. The annual Corruption Perceptions Index, which ranks countries by perceived levels of corruption via surveys and assessments, ranks Pakistan a thirty-two, or "Mostly Corrupt."[1] Even the legal system finds itself divided between secular and Islamic courts.

---

1   Corruptions Percentage Index 2016 at www.transparency.org

Thus the country of Pakistan sits on a turbulent piece of the earth, seemingly in constant turmoil due to geography, economics, religion, history, crime, and politics. Yet it is a beautiful country. Children still play in the streets, families grow and prosper, laughter and joy abound. Like anywhere else, the country is juxtaposed of tears, smiles, sweat, bright colors, fears, and much love.

Thousands of miles from Pakistan, on a street called Sea Isle in Memphis, Tennessee, another juxtapose existed. From the outside, all appeared calm and peaceful, even aesthetically pleasing. Inside, however, it felt as if the world, as if life itself, constantly tipped on an unseen axis. Economics, religion, history, crime, and politics melded together to create unrest, and eventually it would be the source of a heinous crime that would leave so many scarred forever.

# CHAPTER 3

Memphis Police Lieutenant Walter Norris worked in the homicide division. Parking near the house on Sea Isle Street, which was now designated as a crime scene, he paused, as he carefully took it all in before stepping out of the car. It was May 1, 2003, and the rain had stopped, creating that humid atmosphere so familiar to Memphians like Norris. Norris, an African American with short, dark hair and a slight mustache, turned his head slowly as he reviewed the scene, smoothing the front of his trousers. He quietly conferred with a uniformed Memphis officer who directed the detective to two civilians on a lawn directly across the street. Norris removed a pen and notebook from his jacket pocket as he approached, studying the two people. An elderly white woman, with an olive-skinned boy of about ten years old, sat on the lawn across from the one story brick home where criminal investigators now worked. Both the woman and boy were crying, the woman's arms around the boy. Another woman was in the process of applying a cold rag to the elderly woman's forehead as she whispered soothing words.

Norris, a thirty-year veteran of the Memphis Police Department, had been appointed supervisor of this crime scene. He recognized plenty of faces. He saw the Shelby County Medical Examiner, Dr. O.C. Smith, and they nodded at one another. Yellow crime scene tape was now lifted around the perimeter of the brick home, fluttering in the wind, as officers moved slowly and deliberately. Neighbors were stepping out of their homes into the evening air, gathering in small groups with their arms folded, shifting side to side, as people often do when debating the arrival of so many police cars in so little time.

Now Lieutenant Norris walked across the street to the quaking woman and young boy, smiled softly in an attempt to put them at ease, and introduced himself. He tried to speak to the little boy, but the boy was so traumatized he could not remember his name, where he lived, nor his phone number.

The woman managed to say, "I'm Ernestine Marsh, and this," she hugged the boy tightly, "is my grandson, Jordan."

"You're the one who called the police?"

"Yes. I used the neighbor's phone to dial 9-1-1."

Norris nodded, writing in his notepad. "What's your address?" Ernestine gazed off towards the crime scene, lips quivering. Her eyes fixated on the house.

"Ma'am?" Norris asked again. "What's your address?" Ernestine swayed, caught herself, and looked at her shoes. "I … I don't remember."

"What's your phone number?"

She ran her hand slowly through her hair. "Ah…"

Norris recognized shock, and knew it was normal in these circumstances, so he gave her a few minutes before gently asking, "What happened?"

"We haven't heard from Jordan's father in a while, so we came by to check, and Jordan wanted to get his chicken."

"Chicken?"

"He has a pet chicken in the backyard," the woman wiped away tears with a trembling hand. "And we went to the backyard, and looked in the …" She took a deep breath. "We saw someone in there."

Across the road, crime scene investigators set the scene for their work, opening kits and removing evidence bags.

"Who lives there?" Norris asked gently.

"Jordan's father, my ex-son-in-law Ejaz Ahmad," the woman continued, wiping her nonstop tears, "and his wife, Leah."

Lieutenant Norris conferred with Memphis Police Officers Littlejohn and Leake, who confirmed they had arrived to the call on Sea Isle Road at 5:50 p.m. and met with Mrs. Marsh. Tearfully, she had told them how she had discovered a dead body in the shed. Mrs. Marsh, whose colorful history includes processing crime scenes as a former police officer, was now listed as the complainant. On May 2, their report would include the following information:

VICTIM #1:

Name: Ahmad, Ejaz

Negligent Manslaughter/ Homicide Aggravated Assault Circumstance:

LOVERS QUARREL

Victim Relationship to Suspect:

Offender 1: BOYFRIEND OR GIRLFRIEND[2]

Now at least twelve officers were assigned to secure the crime scene, keep the curious at bay, and ensure the home was undisturbed for the team to gather evidence.

Norris ducked under the crime scene tape to make his way to the back yard. Someone pointed out a square metal shed, missing its sliding door, where it sat on a flat, square concrete pad. It was the inexpensive type, the kind used to store lawn equipment. Norris nodded; his cop's nose told him what was in there before he even approached.

There was something on the ground that looked like latex gloves, located just outside of the shed's door. Upon closer inspection, Norris saw it was actually pieces of skin from human hands.

The body had not been moved, and the crime scene photographer was snapping photographs.

Norris's eyes traveled slowly across the inside of the shed. To one side, two car doors and a motorcycle lay against the inside wall. A square bale of hay sat nearby. The shelves along the sides of the shed were simple planks of wood, some placed haphazardly on top of the other for stability. The inside of the shed had rust stains bleeding down to the floor. There was such a mishmash of junk in the shed that it was difficult to sort it out. An old cash register. A car headlight. Boxes warped with age and dampness. Empty coffee cans,

2    Incident Report #0305000349ME, Memphis Police Department, Entered 05/02/2003

electrical cords. A long white box with "Master Tak" printed on the sides. The shed was not maintained; there was no organization. Whoever owned it was not concerned with neatness or cleanliness. This was a place where unwanted items were stored, items to be saved for "some day." The sole exceptions were the human remains on the floor, and even the body looked as if it had been placed there to be retrieved some other time.

The seasoned officer's eyes then rested on the victim. The nude body was that of a male, the mottled colors of partially decomposed flesh, laying in a fetal position on its right side as if dumped. It was lying about six feet into the shed. The victim was wearing a red and white checked Oxford style shirt that was stiff with body fluids and dirt. It had been hidden under an eggshell foam mattress, and underneath the body was a black plastic garbage bag. The right arm and left leg were stretched out, parallel to the shed door. The left arm, bent at the elbow, lay folded over the right arm. One of the lower arms had been stripped of flesh from elbow to wrist. Rodents had done the work.

The right leg was bent at the knee. There was a wire cable wrapped around one of the legs, and Norris could see, as he turned his head, a red rope tied around one of the victim's arms. He was only mildly surprised to find, in the back corner of the shed, a black and white speckled chicken bobbing its head and watching Norris with a wary eye.

The hen was not the sole live inhabitant. A huge rat was sitting atop the body, boldly glaring at Norris.

Norris hitched his trousers to kneel down, trying to see under and around the body, steadying himself by placing his fingertips on the lawn.

Medical Examiner O.C. Smith soon joined Norris. "What can you tell so far?" Norris asked him.

Smith knelt down to point. "I don't see a lot of insect activity, so I don't think he's been out here long." He shifted his weight. "Judging by the decomposition, I would guess, right now, he's been in here for about two to three weeks."

Norris nodded and both men stood. "Have you been inside the home?"

"Not yet."

"So," Norris asked, flipping his notepad open, "where is the victim's head?"

# CHAPTER 4

Bonnie Garrett was at home when her phone rang at about 5:30 p.m. She answered and immediately recognized the voice of her mother. What Ernestine told her made Bonnie's heart thump wildly.

"I'm with Jordan," Ernestine's voice was coming in gasps. "We're at Ejaz's house ..."

"Did you find him?" Bonnie had been so worried about her ex-husband, and the family had been searching for him all month.

"We found a body," Ernestine was crying. "Bonnie, hurry! Hurry! I think it's Ejaz..."

A white adult female with a bob of red hair arrived on the scene, parking her car across the street from Ejaz's home. She walked up to the crime scene tape, shoulders bowed through the light rain and chilly wind. She wrapped her jacket closer while introducing herself to the officers as the ex-wife of the man who lived at this house. She told Lieutenant Norris her name was Bonnie Garrett and her ex-husband, Ejaz Ahmad, had been missing for some time. In her southern twang, she pronounced the name "Eee-jahz." She explained that Ernestine Marsh was her mother, and Jordan was Ejaz and Bonnie's only son. Jordan's Islamic name was Tariq. "Ejaz is from Pakistan," Bonnie told Norris.

"My mother talked to the neighbor across the street," Bonnie crossed her arms tight. "And I talked to her, too. She said Leah's had a Ryder truck here all week, moving stuff, and all the cars were towed off. Leah told the neighbor that Ejaz had gone to Pakistan and that Leah couldn't afford the house note alone so she ... sir, what happened?" Her voice was quaking. "Is Ejaz ... is it Ejaz?"

Norris was jotting down notes as he spoke with Bonnie. "We haven't identified the victim," he said carefully. "But we'll take prints and compare them to his passport, his other identification papers, to see if it is Mr. Ahmed."

"I can identify him," Bonnie assured him.

"No ma'am, that won't be necessary." He turned to Ernestine Marsh. "Why don't you take your family home, try to get some rest. There's not much you can do here except let us do our work."

Bonnie was adamant. "If you just let me see him! I can tell you if it's him!" She stood on the tips of her toes and craned her neck towards the backyard. "Does he have dark hair? Brown eyes?"

"Miss ..."

"Let me see him! I can identify him!" She was getting near hysterical now. "Does he have dark hair?"

Lieutenant Norris steadfastly looked Ernestine in the eyes. With a deliberate tone he repeated, "Why don't you take your family home." This time it was not a question.

Ernestine Marsh knew then exactly what was being said – and what was not being said. She had been the first female police officer in a tiny town in Florida where her husband was the police chief. She had done a lot of investigating, and was trained to process crime scenes. She nodded understandingly at Norris, put her arm around her daughter. "Let's go, Bonnie," she said gently, reaching for Jordan's hand.

But rather than leave, they sat in Bonnie's car, parked across the street, silently listening to the rain patter on the windows. Bonnie sat in the backseat, trying to remain focused and calm. The two women, normally chattering and gregarious, were now silent as stones.

The investigators knew they would be working their preliminary investigation well into the night. Neighbors were interviewed, and several offered that they had observed a moving van with a few African American men and one white woman moving furniture out of the house a week or so prior to this date.

Looking through the windows, Norris could see the

house was trashed, and there was little furniture. Even the walls were bare. A few items were left behind, nothing of monetary value. Someone had either moved out in a hurry, or there had been a very busy burglar who did not care what he or she took.

The rear sliding glass doors were initially found unlocked; the team made their entry and exit from these doors. A door made of black metal burglar bars covered the main entrance, the front door facing Sea Isle. Trying this front door, Lt. Norris found it locked. He checked all of the outside windows and doors slowly and carefully. There were no signs of a forced entry, no broken glass, no door or window frames showing any sign of marks where someone may have tried to force them open.

Officers were taking possible blood samples from various areas inside the home. They wore masks around their lower faces because the odor, particularly in one of the bedrooms and in the bathroom, was horrible. Again, Norris knew the smell as he entered the home. He walked the inside perimeters, carefully scanned the interior doorframes, handles, and doors for any sign of forced entry, mark, or cuts; there were none. Nor had the windows been tampered with or broken from the inside. All of the door locks were in good condition, none were broken, nor showed any signs of having been punched or jimmied.

Investigators continued to gain access into the house from the backyard, carefully sliding open the rear sliding glass door off the patio. From here, they stepped into what appeared to be a den or living room area. The beige carpet was dirty; there were two desks in the room, and a clear chandelier was hanging from the ceiling. Three large boxes full of trash were in this room. The lights from the flashing camera bounced off bare walls.

Peeking into one of the boxes, an investigator noted a half-eaten yellow and white sheet cake among the papers and trash, the kind of cake that came on a flat cardboard ordered from a local market. The plastic cover for the cake lay on the kitchen floor.

One investigator carefully opened the drawers of the desks, which were all empty.

A few knife sheaths, minus the knives, were located and photographed. A sword leaned against one wall; a large, circular knife was found between a desk and the wall.

A search of the kitchen cabinets revealed nothing of notable interest to the crime scene investigators, only spices, pots, pans, utensils, and nonperishable food.

Similar to so many other American kitchens, this kitchen's refrigerator served as the home's bulletin board. Officers copied down the information from the flyers and notes posted on the refrigerator. There was a note that appeared to be information for an appointment at Medical Psychiatric Associates, and a flyer from the Baptist College of Health Sciences with several names written on the flyer, including a "Muhammad Asif." Mail retrieved from the kitchen trash was addressed to Ejaz Ahmad at that residence address.

A medium-sized storage room was off the left of the kitchen. The only items in the room were two vacuum cleaners, boxes, and unrelated items. Some junk had been pushed up into one of the corners: a pair of blue and white shoes, a plastic milk crate, a piece of old foam, some boxes. "According to his ex-mother-in-law, the victim kept the items for his store in this room," an officer told Norris.

"His what?"

"He had a shop where he sold stuff, stuff brought over from Pakistan."

In what appeared to serve as the living room, the carpet had been pulled up from the floor. A book titled "The Noble Qur'an" lay on the floor. The room was bare of furnishings. In a small alcove there were clothing hangers, videotapes, and an unopened energy drink. An investigator pointed out the living room door. "Someone's tried to clean this, but you can tell where they didn't do a good job." Photos were taken; notes were carefully made.

A hallway led out of the living room to several bedrooms and a bathroom. "They tried to clean this, too," an officer noted, pointing at the floor with a gloved hand. "See the trail between the bathroom and the living room? Like a dirty mop was dragged along."

The first bedroom was smaller than the others, and the odor of death seeped into the nostrils of the investigative team. A used condom lay on the floor near a window. Also on the floor was an ATM card from Bank of America, a child's drawing, and a piece of paper with a number written across it.[3] A telephone cord was wrapped up in one corner. Perusing the closet, investigators noted some hangers and men's clothing. None of these items were proof of the crime, so they were not confiscated as evidence.

The bathroom was small, with just enough space for one or two people to move around but still having to lean away to allow the other room. The fixtures were the aqua blue of the time period it was built, with a newer wooden toilet seat. The bathroom was bare, but the stench was strongest in this room. A yellow liquid, including several strands of hair, trailed from the bathroom door to the closed lid of the toilet. There were two stains in the checked white tile, the largest being a brown color directly in front of the vanity. The small medicine cabinet, bolted to the wall over the vanity, was empty. From this angle it was evident someone had tried to clean up, and then dragged a dirty mop from the bathroom, down the hall, and into the kitchen. Still, the bottom doorframe held older dirt in the crevices. A thin, sticky film of dirty residue clung to the insides of the tub.

Investigators worked room to room. Like the others, the second bedroom was void of furnishings. A backpack was located on a shelf in the closet; it contained various books on electronics. A packet of tools, some pieces of green material,

3  The condom and the ATM card were not considered evidence

and a long black belt all lay scattered on the floor.

The third bedroom did not yield much either, mainly a computer monitor and a small television. On the floor near the closet were two keys, a lighter, and a small laundry basket. A bag of hangers was located inside the closet.

The bed remained in the master bedroom, stripped of linens. The bare mattress set and frame were all that was left. Carpet in the bedroom had been cut or torn away from some areas, all the way down to the concrete pad. It appeared as if someone had clearly tried to cover his or her tracks.

Judging by what they saw and what they knew of crime scenes, the team wondered if the master bedroom was the "primary" crime scene, with the shed being a "dump site."

Outside of the home, there were various bills in the mailbox postmarked April 29th. A cigar stub was located near the front door.

When it was time to remove the body from the shed, Norris and Dr. Smith stood by as the remains were carefully removed and placed into a body bag. Because of decomposition, there remained skin tissue on the shed's concrete pad. "It's from the victim's hand," Dr. Smith pointed out.

"It's possible we can lift it, get a good print for identification purposes," Dr. Smith said. He slipped on a latex glove, popping it tight across one hand. Carefully, he slid the gloved hand into the skin. It was as if he now wore two gloves on one hand.

When the body was moved, another discovery was made. The victim's penis and scrotum were missing.

Crime scene investigators told Norris about the few swords found in the home. They had been photographed, bagged into evidence, and tagged with all necessary information.

Dr. Smith joined Norris and they walked through the house, speaking quietly together, taking notes. Occasionally one of the men would point at something and they would stop to look carefully. Once evidence is gone, it is gone forever, and anything and everything had to be carefully scrutinized.

Hours later, Bonnie, Ernestine, and Jordan watched from the parked car, in a daze, as an empty gurney was wheeled to the back of the house. She watched while the gurney reappeared, a black body bag atop the crisp white of the gurney's linens.

Bonnie's world, along with everyone else who loved Ejaz, now became a "before" and "after" life, divided in just a few seconds. She knew in her heart who was in that body bag. She does not remember the ride home.

Finally, the crime scene was placed under security overnight, and the team planned to return in the morning to finish processing the scene.

Investigators continued canvassing the neighborhood to ask questions and take notes. They knew it would be hard to miss the smell coming from the backyard shed, but due to wind and temperatures it could be difficult to discern the source. There had been a lot of rain in April, with temperatures dropping to the forties at night and rising to the mid-eighties during the day.

The crime was shocking to the neighbors. This was not an area where finding a dumped body was normal. This was not a rough area of Memphis; there were no vacant homes with boarded windows or people wandering the street looking for trouble. It was an area where, while the ranch style homes were older, they were not dilapidated, and the yards were well kept. People cared about themselves and their property, even the streets were clear of debris. This evil that had invaded the quiet street was a rare intrusion. But then, some neighbors told each other, this *was* Memphis.

# CHAPTER 5

*The thing about Memphis is that it's pleasingly off-kilter.*
*Historian & Author Hampton Sides*

Memphis has a myriad of characteristics that give it much personality, in part due to its history.

In the 1500s, explorers from Spain and France visited the area, and in the 1680s French explorers built Fort Prudhomme in the vicinity. It was a prime spot, owing to the fertile soil and the nearby Mississippi River.

The Chickasaw Native Americans had already made their home on the banks of the river. It is believed they had migrated from western regions to west of the Mississippi River in the 1300s. The powers that were about to invade their world did not care where they were from, only that they needed to be gone, thus the Chickasaw nation was forced, via the Indian Removal Act of 1830, to cede their land to the United States government. Later, in 1837, the Chickasaws would be forced to march away from Memphis, Tennessee, which marked the beginning of the infamous Trail of Tears, crossing back over the Mississippi river, where they ultimately settled in Oklahoma.

The original Memphis, founded in 1819 by a group of investors including Andrew Jackson, the then President of the nation, was four blocks wide with about fifty inhabitants. It was a desirable area, sitting on the banks of the Mississippi, a prime location for a port and trading center. It was named after the capitol of Egypt, which also rested on the lip of a mighty and life-sustaining river.

The Irish and the Germans flooded in, building homes, churches, and businesses, as they settled into their life as Americans.

Slave labor built the roads, farmed the land, and worked

construction. The Civil War divided the country; the city of Memphis was divided as well. At the time, slavery was believed by many to be a necessary commodity, but nonetheless, Memphis still maintained strong industrial ties to the north. When the Yankees won the Battle of Shiloh, in the bloodiest battle in American history, over twenty-three thousand casualties later, General Grant plunked down a flag to base Union headquarters in the town.

Memphis' signature dish, barbeque, is believed to have been introduced to the Caribbean and Americas by Spanish explorers or African slaves who are credited with the process of using spices and sauces in order to make edible the worst cuts of meat. Memphis is known for its barbeque.

In 1812, the people along the shores of the Mississippi River gazed, with slack jaws, as the waters surged backward. The phenomenon lasted several hours; it was caused by possibly the strongest earthquake in history. It is still discussed today. Yet it was not the worst occurrence on the Mississippi near Memphis.

On April 27, 1865, the *S.S. Sultana* side-wheel steamboat exploded seven miles away from the Memphis shores. The fire could be seen from the town's Mud Island. It was the worst maritime disaster in U.S. history, with 1,800 people dead, surpassing the loss of life from the *RMS Titanic* sinking. The majority of the 2,427 passengers were Union soldiers released from prison and on their way home, traveling in a boat with a legal maximum capacity of 376. Bodies of victims floated as far away as Vicksburg. Wreckage would be discovered as late as 1982.

In 1878, the Memphis population was at 47,000, but yellow fever wiped out more than 5,000 people, with at least 27,000 folks packing up and heading out. Those who were left discovered a new sewage system and the natural artesian wells; the latter would halt the plague. These hardcore Memphis residents dug in their heels to stay. Fifteen million dollars in losses bankrupted the city; but Memphis, ever a fighter, hung on.

Memphis has a history of such resilience … and violence. Georgia Tann (1891-1950) a matronly, smiling, elderly woman created and used the Memphis based, unlicensed Tennessee Children's Home Society to run an infamous black-market baby operation. Using illegal means to obtain "marketable" babies, Tann and her cohorts obtained and sold the children by false paperwork, theft, kidnap, deception, and extortion. She hired a staff of molesters and abusers. Babies who did not sell were murdered. Tann exchanged babies and monetary gifts with Memphis police, judges, and elected officials for political favors and legal protection. Thousands of children were murdered or sold; notable buyers included actress Joan Crawford and New York Governor Herbert Lehman. Operating successfully from the 1920s to 1950, Tann was never prosecuted. Tann's legacy continues to this day in the lives of thousands of people who have no idea of their true heritage because it was all stolen from them.[4]

Memphis is home to significant musical claims to fame. Sun Records is a recording studio that is not much to look at, but the artists who walked through its doors would come to be watched by millions of people. Elvis Presley purchased a Memphis home in 1957 that would later become the vacation destination of up to six hundred thousand tourists a year (the second most visited residence in the United States, surpassed only by the White House). Stax Records, established in 1957, produced almost exclusively black performers. Such names as Howlin' Wolf, Muddy Waters, and B.B. King grace the labels on the vinyl discs. Memphis is also known as "Home of the Blues."

A Memphis sanitation worker strike brought civil rights to full swing in the 1960s, in a town built by black hands who were not even allowed to enter many of its doors. Dr. Martin Luther King, Jr., arrived in an attempt to quell the fires of anger. Instead, shots rang out at the Lorraine Motel

4   Raymond, B.B. "The Baby Thief." (2007). Carroll & Graf, NY

and one of the greatest leaders in United State's history was gone.

Now riverside areas Beale Street and Mud Island have been refurbished and rebuilt to welcome the hordes of tourists who come to eat barbeque, listen to blues, and tour Graceland. Riverboats continue to chug up and down the Mississippi over the grave of the *S.S. Sultana*. The Lorraine Motel is a civil rights museum where somber visitors stand only a few feet from where Dr. King fell. A thirty seconds drive over the Memphis-Arkansas Bridge takes you over the Mississippi River into Arkansas, the first town after the bridge being West Memphis. Returning from West Memphis at night, the multicolor glow of the reflection of Memphis lights on the river is a breathtaking sight. There are many beautiful areas in Memphis, with its stately homes that have been maintained for decades, lush trees and parks, and lovely public buildings. Many historical places exist, still in proud and stately beauty.

Memphis continues to have its issues, where entire apartment complexes and businesses are abandoned, and in certain neighborhoods if burglar bars don't surround all windows, plywood will. In 2006, Memphis was ranked number one in the nation for violent crimes. In 2001, 2005, 2006, and 2007, it was ranked the second most dangerous U.S. city. The violent crime rate for Memphis in 2012 was higher than the national violent crime rate by 352.41%. Robbery, rape, murder, assault, and theft are crimes that dot the city map like a speckled egg.

It seems, throughout its history, that the city of Memphis was always battling a foe, whether it was Indians, Rebel soldiers, sickness, race, crime, the terrain, or poverty. Perhaps this is what gives its people their survivalist personality. It is said people either love the city or despise it. It is a diverse city, where you rarely find an unfriendly stranger but you can always find something fun to do – "fun" being quite subjective, a night on Beale or a shooting being both potential results.

The arrival on May 1, 2003, of police to the crime scene on Sea Isle Street on that cold afternoon meant another murder, more victims. Hopefully, this would be a case resulting in an arrest with justice for the victim.

# CHAPTER 6

On May 2nd, the day after the discovery of Ejaz's body in the shed, the crime scene unit returned to the home on Sea Isle. Their job was to gather any evidence that was possibly missed on May 1st, with a goal of locating the victim's head.

The officers slid open the glass door at the rear of the home and stepped inside. The smell of a dead body remained evident; it is not a smell easily described or easily forgotten. Investigators wrinkled their noses at the odor.

Immediately, they noted the missing pieces of carpet in the living room and the hallway. The crime scene investigators had also removed some carpet in the hopes of finding blood or any other evidence. "The Locard Principle" was in effect.

Dr. Edmond Locard, a forensic pioneer in the late 1800s, applied theoretical ideology to crime scene examination. Dr. Locard created the basic principal of "every contact leaves a trace." Simply applied, it means that all those entering a room will leave evidence such as dirt, skin follicles, hair, body fluids, and prints. Leaving the room, the person will carry with them fibers, soil, or liquids, anything that will cling to their clothing, hair, or skin. It was hoped, on this day of May 2nd, that investigators would find answers via "The Locard Principle."

Now investigators located dark stains on the floor in the living room. Using their crime scene kit, they took swab samples of this stain in order to send it to a lab in an effort to determine if it was blood. There were more stains in the hallway and on walls and doors. The bathroom floor yielded a colored liquid on the tile floor. Investigators ensured they had samples from each place. They also took "control samples," or swabs from areas where nothing suspicious existed. The control samples would be matched to the suspicious samples. A crime scene photographer took photos. Another investigator measured and made a diagram of the interior of the house. All of the evidence samples were bagged, sealed, labeled, and later taken to the police department evidence room where they were inventoried.

A gentleman arrived, parked his vehicle, and approached an officer standing outside guarding the scene. The man explained he was friends with Ejaz Ahmad, but had not seen Ejaz for months; they worshipped at the same Mosque. "I spoke to him about a month ago," the man explained. "Ejaz told me he was having really bad problems with his wife."

"His wife?"

"Well, she is his wife; they are married as part of a religion only," the man explained in his clipped accent.

The officer took down the man's contact information, and told the gentleman that a sergeant would contact him. .

The wailing of Bonnie Garrett and her family drowned out the television news. They cried into their hands, falling against one another on the couch. Ernestine Marsh, Bonnie, and Bonnie's sister Johnny Joy grabbed on to one another as life preservers, drowning in their tears. The pictures on television were of Ejaz's home, the address just out of camera sight. They could see the crime scene investigators in their jumpsuits, dodging under the crime scene tape to walk to the back yard. The red and blue lights from the police cruisers occasionally streaked across the home.

They did not see the picture on the television; it was a blur. All they heard was that Ejaz Ahmad was found in his shed … beheaded.

It was the first time any of them knew he had been beheaded. Bonnie broke away from her family to race, stumbling, to the bathroom. She made it just in time to vomit into the commode. It felt like everything in her system was falling out of her body into the toilet, including her heart.

# CHAPTER 7

The word "autopsy" comes from the Latin word *autopsia* meaning, literally, "an eye witnessing." The origin is Greek "seeing with one's own eyes." *Autos* being "self,'" *opis* "a sight." The ancient Egyptians dissected bodies to prepare them for the afterlife, but the 1670s introduced the first written recordings of dissection for the sole purpose of determining cause of death.

The autopsy performed on Ejaz Ahmad on June 16, 2003, was for the sole purpose of determining cause of death.

Forensic Pathologist Dr. Teresa Campbell is board certified in Anatomical and Clinical Pathology, Family Practice, and Forensic Pathology. A graduate of the Medical University of South Carolina, she was assigned to perform the autopsy on the victim, to "see with her own eyes." The anatomic diagnosis determined two gunshot wounds to the chest, a "contusion in the left upper lobe of lung, sharp force injuries to the neck and left upper leg, (and) moderate decomposition." Dr. Campbell noted there were knife wounds on the body, but she could not determine if the wounds had been made before or after death.

Dr. Campbell had ordered x-rays of the body. Now, examining them carefully, she observed a spent bullet over the spine. She noted the track from the bullet's entry into the body to where it came to rest. The bullet had traveled downward on a left to right path; on its way it had pierced the heart's left ventricle, through the diaphragm and stomach, coming to rest in the tissues lying over the spine, where Dr. Campbell removed it.

The "small caliber, hollow point, copper washed bullet" was noted, retrieved, photographed, and placed in an evidence bag to be marked and sealed for the forensics department.

There were multiple stab wounds to the neck area where

the head had been removed, leaving a pattern of jagged skin. It was theorized that the stab wounds were the perpetrator's attempt to locate where to cut off the head. Some of the stab wounds measured up to 1.1 inches long and 2.1 inches deep.

"Sharp force injury to the left hip, abdomen, and perineum (the area between the scrotum and the anus)" measuring 10 by 8.5 inches was noted, exposing the femur head. *(The femoral head is located between the femur (thigh bone) and the hip socket. The femoral neck is between the femur head and the femur.)* The edges were mostly round except the lateral edge, "rounded with a sharp defect." Over the right hip, a second cut measured 3.3 by 1.5 inches.

Dr. Campbell noted that "The penis and scrotum are absent." Was this due to the perpetrator's apparent and crude attempt to remove the leg, or was the removal something more sinister, perhaps as an act of retribution?

Despite decomposition, Dr. Campbell was able to determine the body had been moved from a "protected area" – one that shielded it from the elements - by judging the marks and internal organs.

Dr. Jennifer Love, a forensic anthropologist, has three main duties: skeletal recovery, forensic anthropology services, and identification. She was called in to work the case. Peering through her black-framed glasses, her angular face a study of determination; she scrutinized the victim's bones.

It was Love's duty to try and assess the victim's age, sex, ethnicity, and any identifying marks on the bones that would tell what occurred to cause or aid the demise. As a member of the Harris County Institute of Forensic Science, Dr. Love also works with The Doe Network, a nonprofit organization whose goal was to identify unclaimed bodies and skeletal remains. She is an expert in her work.

Dr. Love discovered a marking, indicative of a cut by a sharp-edged knife, on the cervical vertebrae, the bone located at the back of the neck. There was also a marking on the victim's left femoral head indicating someone had attempted to cut off the leg. Markings on the victim's forearm, Dr. Love determined, were consistent with rodent activity.

It appeared someone had tried to dismember the body with at least three different sharp instruments of an unknown type.

The results of the "possible blood samples" which had been taken from the house were returned from the crime lab. There was no presence of blood.

The skin tissue carefully removed by Coroner O.C. Smith from the concrete pad of the shed positively identified the victim as Ejaz Ahmad.

# CHAPTER 8

Walter Norris read an advertisement in 1974 that the Memphis Police Department was hiring "Capable Blacks." Bemused, he wondered what a "Capable Black" was, exactly. He had served four years in the Army, 1966 to 1969, as part of the 87th Airborne at Fort Bragg. "I guessed that qualified as 'capable,' and I am black" he now chuckles. Norris put in his application and was hired that year. Norris would eventually work "Organized Crime, Vice, Robbery, Homicide, really just everywhere," he recalled. A stint in Internal Affairs led to a Commander position. By 2003, Norris had worked over nine hundred homicide cases. He was most affected by cases involving the murder of children. He saw enough cases of boyfriends murdering their girlfriend's children to know not everyone has a parental instinct. A case he worked involving the murder of two elderly women by a man on parole continues to be difficult to discuss; the man had murdered a ninety-one year old woman and her neighbor, who was in her seventies. "The man even killed the victim's little dog," Norris remembers with a catch in his voice.

Norris was born and raised in Memphis, a city he loves and admits "has its share of problems." As a boy, he had caused some of those problems with his own criminal behavior. "Anyone can solve a problem," he philosophizes, "but they have to work together to do it."

Now Norris was working to solve the mystery of Ejaz Ahmad's demise, looking for whoever had information leading to the crime. He went to the Mosque where Ejaz had worshipped and questioned people. Most spoke Urdu as their native tongue, the national language of Pakistan, but they also spoke English.

"We have not seen Ejaz for several weeks," his friends told Norris. One of them had a phone number in Pakistan, someone who could either reach Ejaz or knew him well enough to know if he had visited there recently. Norris called the number and soon discovered Ejaz had not been to Pakistan in a long time.

The investigators learned Ejaz once owned a shop in the Memphis Mall where he sold, among other items, swords and bladed weapons. The shop was called Regal Imports. He flew to Pakistan to purchase items and brought them to Tennessee to sell. Sometimes he bought items from a friend who had a warehouse full of items from Pakistan. He also dabbled in selling used cars. Ejaz was obviously a hard worker, with a myriad of business ventures to include rental homes, car sales, and retail. Investigators learned he was an educated man who held two Master's Degrees in Engineering, having completed his Bachelors Degree while still a teenager.

In order to find out who murdered him, the investigators knew to look inside his closest circle, beginning by first looking at family, then close friends. Statistics told them there was an eighty percent chance the culprit was in this circle.

Thus, the Memphis investigators began to put puzzle pieces together to find out: Who was Ejaz Ahmad?

# CHAPTER 9

*He had such a thirst for knowledge.*
*Ejaz's son, Jordan (Tariq) Ahmad*

"Ejaz was the kindest man I have ever known," Ernestine Marsh says with conviction. "He was modest, he was kind, and he had manners." Ernestine is a tough judge of character. She was born in 1930, and her family hails from the tiny town of Dyers, Arkansas, the birthplace of singer Johnny Cash. Ernestine told how, in her youth, a girlfriend talked her into going to the Dyers drug store to meet two boys; the teenagers met a quiet young man named John and his friend in a corner booth. They sipped sodas and chatted with the future megastar performer. Ernestine's father was a best friend of Vernon Presley; she can remember visiting Vernon and Gladys Presley and their little boy, Elvis. Ernestine has been divorced once and widowed twice ("Both times to Texas men," she said), and was the first policewoman in Pahokee, Florida, where her husband was Police Chief during the racial riots of the 1950s. Some of her music has been recorded professionally and used in films. She loves to dress fashionably, and she loves hats. "You don't let a hat wear you," she advises, "*you* wear the hat." She has considered writing a book on her adventurous life. "Honey, I can tell you some stories," she says. "I can talk the horns off a billy goat." One of her favorite topics is her ex-son-in-law, Ejaz Ahmad. Being a history buff and after having long talks with Ejaz about his life, Ernestine happily recalls the story of how Ejaz came to America.

World War II had ended, and Muslims from British India objected to uniting with India. Muslims moved to Pakistan, the new nation. It was not safe, so in order to escape the Indian army, Sohoi Hafeez Ahmad and his wife Aziza had their family pack quickly. What could not be packed on the cart was left behind. Aziza took a needle and thread, then scooped up her jewelry. To keep these heirlooms safe, she sewed the pieces into the hems of her clothing.

Sohoi Hafeez told his family he was going to go ahead of them to the Lyallpur District in an effort to find them a home and work. Pakistan was a new nation; there were many opportunities. When his family arrived, they found him sitting on a piece of property, staking his claim. Once the town was established, he filed ownership of the property to legally register it.

The Ahmad family prospered with hard, honest work. Soon they owned an entire block of numerous businesses. Their apartment was located on the second story over one of the shops.

The Lyallpur District was renamed Faisalabad, after King Faisal of Saudi Arabia. It grew to be the third largest metropolitan area in Pakistan. It became a road and railway center, where fifty-five percent of Pakistan's exports were grown: wheat, cotton, sugarcane, fruits, and vegetables. It has unforgiving climates; in summer, the thermometer may soar up to 122 degrees Fahrenheit between May and July. In winter, the temperature can drop to a bone-chilling 28 degrees during the months of December, January, and February.

Ejaz Ahmad was born in Faisalabad on February 8, 1962, the baby among numerous older siblings. When Sohoi Hafeez died, Aziza was left with the work of raising the family and running the household. She took in sewing, and she performed odd jobs to keep food on the table and a roof over the family. Ejaz learned the value of hard work from his parents, particularly his mother. The family spoke Urdu, their native tongue. They were a handsome family, with dark hair, dark eyes, and olive skin.

One night Ejaz's mother woke him from a deep sleep. "I need to talk to you," Aziza told her 18-year-old son. A bit confused, his eyes full of sleep, he followed her out to the veranda over their store, and each took a chair.

"I have saved and saved money for you," Ejaz's mother told him. "I want you to use it, to go to America and get a good education."

Ejaz stifled a yawn. "Mother, why are you telling me this now? I was asleep!"

"Listen to me," she gripped his hand. "It is my dream. You go to America and go to college."

Ejaz was a bit confused. He had been attending school in Pakistan, and now held a Bachelor's Degree.

"Promise me," she insisted.

He nodded slowly, and then he saw a strange light in her eyes.

"I love you," she said, and slumped over in his arms.

"Mother!" He shook her. "Mother! What is it?"

As he held her and sobbed, Ejaz knew she was gone forever. Her body lay motionless across his heaving chest. Ejaz held his mother tightly, tears flowing down his face. "I promise, mother," he managed to say. "I promise!"

She had died from a heart attack. Ejaz's mother followed him in his dreams for the rest of his life.

Aziza had been quietly setting aside money for his American trip, money she should have been spending on herself. Ejaz granted his mother her last wish, and kept his promise to set out to attend college in the United States.

Ejaz first attended a language school in Alabama, where it cost him $1,500 to learn to speak English. Later, he would become fluent in several languages. In addition to his native language Urdu, Ejaz spoke French, English, and some Arabic. He grew to be a bit over six feet tall, lanky, and handsome. His smile was blindingly white, and his eyes danced with happiness.

Ejaz moved into an apartment in Memphis with a friend named Jimmy. They worked, attended college classes, and spent time cooking, laughing, and talking while at home. Initially, he went to the University of Mississippi, affectionately known as "Ole Miss," to attend college and training. Afterwards, he transferred his credits to Memphis State College. He would eventually hold two master's Degrees in the field of engineering.

One day in 1992, Ejaz was riding with a friend who also gave a ride to a man named Johnny Smith, Jr. Johnny and Ejaz began talking. Johnny liked Ejaz right away; he was kind, funny, and a perfect gentleman. Ejaz liked Johnny as well; they were close in age, and they shared the same old-fashioned values. Soon Johnny was joining other friends at Ejaz's apartment. Johnny pronounced his friend's name "Eee-jazz" in his strong Southern drawl. "Ejaz was an excellent cook," Johnny recalled. The group often sat around talking and laughing. The fragrant aroma of curry and spices wafted from Ejaz's kitchen where he regularly cooked dishes of beef, chicken, or lamb, stirring it together with rice. His friends continually glanced into the kitchen, anxiously wondering when it would be time to eat.

One of the favorite things the group of friends enjoyed doing when they gathered at Ejaz's home for a meal was watching Pakistani movies. Ejaz had a favorite, called "Sometimes Happy, Sometimes Sad" (*Kabhi Khushi Kabhie Gham*). It is the story of a young man who meets and falls in love with a woman from the lower class. Against his traditional father's wishes and refusal to give his blessing, the couple runs away. It is, just as the title suggested, a funny movie with laughter, and a sad movie with tears. Ejaz watched it over and over.

Slowly, Ejaz began to accumulate businesses, some he co-owned with friends. In addition to owning rental property and selling used cars, he owned two gas stations and a fish market where people came to purchase fresh seafood, or to get a bite to eat at the small restaurant attached to the business. Later, he was known to always have several thousand dollars in cash on him. Sometimes he hid the money in his home, often under a desk.

He was not in the States long when Ejaz discovered peanut butter. The minute he tried it, "he went crazy for it," recalls a close friend. Ejaz smeared peanut butter on everything he could. He raved about how good it was, and how everyone should try it. "He ate peanut butter for months," laughed his friend. "And that was it. He got so sick of it, he could never eat it again!"

Johnny Smith, Jr., was born and raised in Memphis. He was working in a store when a customer, who wore a long shirt and a strange looking hat, came in asking for matches. "What religion are you?" the gregarious Johnny asked him.

They began talking and the man invited Johnny to the Mosque. "I thought that was just a big mansion!" Johnny told him, and they both laughed. He became intrigued when he went to the Mosque and began learning more about the Islamic beliefs. "I was raised Christian," Johnny explained. "Even when I converted to Muslim, I felt, deep down in my heart, I still believed in Christianity." This was in 1990. "Islam appealed to me at the time." Johnny took a Muslim name and worshipped at the mosque.

Ejaz did not have much money, but what he lacked in finances he made up for with ambition and creativity. He and Johnny would load up his white Ford van and set up on a street corner in a high-traffic area. They sold items such as bicycles, jackets, and decorative pictures. "Ejaz was a good salesman," Johnny recalled, as he described how his friend had started small and eventually built up quite a business. "I mean, he could sell anything!"

Ejaz loved his friends and family, and he loved to laugh and have fun. It seemed the only thing missing in his life was a true romantic love. Many women found Ejaz attractive and exciting, but he abided by strict Muslim tradition. While he was a natural flirt, he was not going to live with someone until he was married and in love. Until then, he focused on his work and friends.

That was about to change.

# CHAPTER 10

It seemed, to Bonnie Marsh, that she could never quite find exactly what she was seeking. That is, until the minute she saw Ejaz Ahmad walk through her mother's living room.

A Pakistani man named Qaiser became smitten with Ernestine Marsh, and he relentlessly pursued her. He was determined to make her love him, so the dark-haired man would just show up, unannounced, at her door. She always let him in and spent time visiting, but she had made it clear she was only interested in friendship.

On one particular day in late January 1988, Qaiser brought a friend. He introduced his friend as Ejaz Ahmad. Ernestine politely welcomed Ejaz into her home, shaking his hand and smiling broadly.

Standing behind her mother, Bonnie could only stare.

She saw a thin, tall, olive-skinned man with thick black hair, combed and nicely styled. He dressed casually but the creases in his shirt and pants were ironed crisply. A shock of curling black chest hair peeped just over the open top button of his oxford style shirt. When Ejaz turned his gaze on her and shook her hand, Bonnie *knew*. She just *knew*.

*"I'm going to marry this man,"* she told herself. She could not stop looking into those dark eyes, eyes that danced with fun and intelligence. When she finally had to step back, she internally shook herself. *"What the hell,"* she demanded of herself as her mother prattled on in the background, *"are you thinking?"*

Bonnie already had enough problems, she decided, without letting a crush get in the way. She was working two jobs to eke by, as a cashier in a casino and as a telemarketer, a job she loathed but needed for the money. She had a son, Drake, by her first husband, a Pakistani man who was also handsome and charming, but wanted nothing to do with fatherhood and marriage.

She was a pretty girl, with sparkling eyes; just barely over 5' tall, she wore her reddish brown hair in a short bob. Still, it always seemed like she attracted the wrong type of guys. She had too many things going on and too many things to sort out in her life, she decided, forcing herself back to reality. No time for love or silly romance.

But when Ejaz looked her in the eyes...

When he looked her in the eyes, she could feel a warm rush from her heart spreading to her fingers and toes. She felt she could speak to him without saying anything. His eyes bore into hers, as he smiled at her with his perfect white teeth and deep dimples. Ejaz had a soft voice with strength behind it. He carried himself with self-assurance, not that false bravado she was so tired of seeing in many Southern men.

Ernestine Marsh says it was when Bonnie sang that Ejaz fell in love. Bonnie loved to sing, and Ernestine wanted her to pursue a show business career. So with some encouragement, Bonnie blushed and performed an impromptu number called "Gee Whiz," a song made popular by Carla Thomas in the early 1960's, penned when Thomas was 15 years old. As she belted out the bluesy, soulful tune, Bonnie could have been singing about Ejaz

They went to the movies on their first date. Bonnie shared with him about how she first lived in West Palm Beach, Florida, where she was born, but her family moved to Memphis soon afterwards. When she was four, they moved to Southaven, Mississippi. Sometimes the gregarious, chatty Bonnie found herself stumbling over words. When he looked at her, she felt like the only woman on earth. If their fingers touched it seemed an electrical jolt zapped through her. He was intelligent, witty, and she loved his rich accent. When he laughed it was as if he enjoyed laughing as much as what made him laugh. "I love America!" He would tell her, eyes dancing. His favorite actor, he told Bonnie, was Al Pacino. "I look like him, yes?" Ejaz would ask, patting his jaws as he tilted his head.

"No!" She would giggle.

"Yes, I do!" He would strike a pose. "Just like 'Scarface.'"

He loved her spark, her wit, how she would say whatever she felt. He laughed and shook his head. "Bonnie, the things that come out your mouth!"

He could get angry, and was unafraid to voice his opinion. But there was no door slamming, no screaming, and absolutely no physical hitting or pushing. He and Bonnie were both nonsmokers and teetotalers. Ejaz did not believe in putting those chemicals into the body, and Bonnie just did not care for cigarettes or alcohol, save a few daring sips of beer as a teenager.

In Pakistan, he told her, his sister was a dressmaker and his brother was a jeweler. Ejaz gave Bonnie exquisite, one-of-a-kind dresses and jewelry. He loved to give her these gifts, smiling broadly as she tried them on.

Ejaz took care of Drake. He took him to the mosque, he taught Drake about his culture, history, and included him in their lives together.

Bonnie later confided in a friend, "It was our world, you know? And you're in a place that some people go their whole life without ever finding. Every time I looked at him, I could see how things would be."

Ejaz felt the same way, so, in November 1988, they stopped by Ernestine's house where they found her digging in the flowerbeds with a trowel, the knees of her pants blackened with rich soil.

"Come on," Bonnie tugged her mom's arm to help her stand. "We're going to get married! Come on!"

Ernestine looked down at her old work clothes, the heavy gardener's gloves. "I can't go looking like this!" She mopped her brow, leaving a smudge of dirt across her forehead.

"No!" Ejaz insisted. "You must go with us!"

They waited while Ernestine changed into something suitable. The three drove to Marion, Arkansas, where the

Justice of the Peace performed the ceremony in his office.

Ernestine was ready for a celebration, but Ejaz had to go to St. Louis for work and Bonnie had to go to work immediately after the ceremony. It did not matter; she knew how much they loved one another. A stranger could tell just by the way they looked at one another.

When Ejaz returned, he confessed to his new bride he did not feel their wedding ceremony was right, as he was a Muslim. So again, with Ernestine in tow, the couple went to the mosque for their wedding in traditional Islamic fashion. Ernestine, who worshipped at The Church of Jesus Christ of Latter-Day Saints, found the ceremony interesting and intriguing. The Muslim men and women "were so nice," she recalls in her Southern drawl. "They treated us so good." She learned the wedding ceremony is called a *Nikkah*, and that Islam condoned extravagance, which includes weddings. In true Islamic faith, no one was forced to marry, particularly females, she was told; that was just another myth. She found no prejudice, no discrimination while there.

The Imam performed the ceremony, read the *Nikkah Khutba*, which cites the purpose of marriage as being for a man and woman to trust, love, and be fair to one another.

Bonnie was aware of what people said, and of what some of her peers wondered. Too many Americans assumed, because she was married to a Muslim man, that she was now relegated to being treated as a second class citizen, or that she was not allowed to speak and had to walk behind her husband. "It's not like that," she now explained. "Ejaz never saw me, or any woman, as a 'second class citizen.' When we walked, he wanted me at his side, because side-by-side means you are equal."

People questioned Bonnie's marriage to a Muslim. Didn't Muslims force their wives to cover themselves with a heavy veil and dress? As in any religion, there are traditions in the Islamic religion some outsiders considered strange, or unequal, maybe even frightening. One misinterpretation was the burqa. Bonnie's studies told her that a burqa was worn in only certain regions of the Middle East, and were either politically forced or part of certain religious sects, to include the ultra-Orthodox Jewish Haredi burqas.

"Don't Arab men beat their wives?" a coworker blatantly asked her.

"Men beat their wives in all religions," Bonnie replied. "Ejaz would never lay his hands on me. He is a *true* Muslim man." She told others, "And he does not care I am American. Discrimination is forbidden in the Islamic faith." She was well aware how abuse occurs in all cultures. Her own mother had married abusive men.

She shook her head at people's ignorance, but then reminded herself; plenty of people misinterpret Christianity, too. She loved Ejaz with her heart and mind. She respected him and believed in him. Her feelings were reciprocated.

Despite having such a wonderful man at her side, Bonnie continued to suffer from a low self-esteem. It was very difficult for her to trust. Her father had been abusive; she had grown up in a home where she had learned to trust no one and felt she was unworthy. Her first husband, who was initially wonderful, handsome, and charming, had slowly begun to show his angry side. In addition to being physically abusive, he beat down what little self-esteem she had managed to hold on to. He eventually abandoned Drake and Bonnie, leaving her and their baby to fend for themselves.

After four months of marriage, Bonnie became fearful. What if this was not what she wanted? Would she wake up and find it was all a lie? Would he turn into the man her ex-husband had become? Despite everything, would Ejaz become abusive, demanding … what if his kindness was all an act? All of these fears slowly pushed her back down into depression and fear. A happy relationship was so foreign to her that it seemed improbable. Rather than let anyone know her feelings, Bonnie bolted and filed for divorce. A friend told her to cite "cruel and unusual circumstances" or "abandonment" to hasten divorce proceedings, so she did.

Ejaz was devastated and Bonnie was heartsick. It took some time, and a lot of talking, but they eventually reunited and remarried. It had not been a dream or a lie, she would come to discover, and Ejaz remained the person she fell in love with. He was faithful, he did not drink or smoke, and drugs were out of the question all together. He worked hard, and he loved Drake. He loved her family, and they loved him back. Everything seemed so wonderful.

# CHAPTER 11

It was practical for Bonnie and Ejaz to live with Ernestine, but for Ejaz there were more than just financial reasons to move in with his mother-in-law. Ejaz believed that, as an older widow, Ernestine should not be alone. "She needs someone to take care of her," he told Bonnie. Unlike so many Americans, the young people in Ejaz's culture did not leave the parent's homes as soon as possible. The older generation needed to be cared for, respected, and besides, what if Ernestine was lonely, living alone?

Bonnie was grateful for Ejaz's stance, as she was close to her mother, and it would have been hard for her to leave her.

The newlyweds initially lived with Ernestine and, during this time, Ejaz became a son to Ernestine. He told her his hopes and dreams. He also occasionally complained about his western wife. Ejaz was from a world where women showed little of their bodies in public. "Tell her!" He would tell Bonnie's family, in his distinct accent, regarding the shorts or dresses she wore.

"You have to understand," Bonnie's family told him. "She's a western girl." Bonnie was not wild or promiscuous; she wore her dresses and shorts average length, although some of them were shorter than others. Still, she refused to dress a certain way just because she was a wife.

Ejaz shook his head sometimes, if Bonnie's thigh was showing in certain dresses or shorts, or when her blouse had no sleeves. He was very traditional.

"That's how it is, here in America," Bonnie's sister told Ejaz.

Ernestine loves to learn about new cultures and enjoys talking to people from all walks of life. She told Ejaz of her times as the first female officer in Pahokee, working with her husband, Police Chief Newton Guy Wood. "He was offered bribes all the time but he never took one," she proudly recalled. "He once told me that if he shut his eyes (to the corruption) we'd be millionaires! He cleaned up that town." They moved so Newton could take a job as Chief of Police in Mariana, Arkansas, and then as Assistant Chief in Forrest City, Arkansas. She lost Newton to a heart attack shortly afterward.

Ejaz confided to Ernestine. "My mother again came to me in a dream," he said, as he told her about the dream. They discussed the hidden meanings of the dream, and she asked about his family.

Ejaz and Ernestine also spent time in the kitchen, laughing and talking, as he taught her how to cook Pakistani food. Sometimes Ejaz would shoo her out so he could cook for the family. Flavored rice with pita bread and yogurt was a favorite. Again, the kitchen was filled with the smell of exotic spices, taking Ejaz back to his childhood.

He was not a perfect man, but he was fair. When he discovered a man named Tony owed a friend of his money for some imported items, Ejaz went to Tony, despite Tony's reputation of bullying others, to get what he wanted. "You owe my friend money!" he told Tony angrily.

"I do not owe anything!"

Ejaz stood his ground. "Pay him!"

Tony grabbed the first thing he could, a 2x4 piece of wood. "Get out!"

When Ejaz later confided to Ernestine about the altercation, she was aghast. "You could've been hurt!"

"He would not pay my friend," Ejaz told her. "It was not fair."

He had no issue with standing up to someone who was being unfair. Bonnie is adamant that he was never mean to her. If they argued, it was over silly stuff. The only music Ejaz enjoyed was Pakistani, but Bonnie did not like the high, whining voices or the repeated riffs. To make her point, she stuck her fingers in her ears, scrunched up her face, and slid down in her seat. Then she played her own music: AC/DC,

Patsy Cline, Ray Charles, Bach, Beethoven, or Alice Cooper. One day, when she played a song called "When the Children Cry" by the rock group White Lion, Ejaz decided he liked Western music after all. Before they went to sleep at night, Ejaz used to ask her to sing the song for him.

Ejaz loved scary and violent movies, and characters with guns blazing. He never grew tired of "Scarface," and he raved about Al Pacino; he watched over and over every movie Pacino made. Bonnie enjoyed the Pakistani movies, and she also loved watching "Sometimes Happy, Sometimes Sad." Really, she did not care what they were doing, as long as they were together.

It was not all perfect and happy. Sometimes they squabbled so badly that Ejaz would storm out of the house. He would go stay with a friend, fluffing up a pillow and trying to fit his lanky body onto a couch. Bonnie was not one to be wooed and sweet-talked, but when he called her to apologize, his voice brimming with tears, she found herself wanting him back in her arms immediately.

Sometimes Ejaz was far too clingy. If she wanted to go somewhere, he wanted to tag along. If she wanted to go out with friends, Ejaz would go along. Bonnie felt claustrophobic at times, and she angrily told him so. "Ugh! You're smothering me!"

"But I want to be with you!"

"I have to have time for me, Ejaz!"

He had such difficulty with the concept. He wanted to spend all of his time with her, but Bonnie was a free spirit.

She jokes now that she had only one rival. Ejaz was in love with Diana, Princess of Wales. He complimented her skin, her eyes, the way she carried herself, and her charitable work. He mooned over pictures of her in a magazine. "She is beautiful, yes?" He never tired of asking.

Ejaz was industrious and his employment history was exemplary. He bussed tables at a Memphis bar and restaurant called Bombay Bicycle Club. He worked at Federal Express, hauling and loading boxes into the trucks. He moved up the Federal Express corporate ladder to be an interpreter. Ejaz went into a partnership with a friend to start a fish market. He continued to sell items under a tent on the roadside. While he was working, he also went to school.

Ejaz eventually opened his own store, Regal Imports, in a small shop in a local mall. It was not long until the shop expanded to a larger place. It featured Pakistani furniture, pictures, lamps, and home furnishings. It also featured beautifully ornate swords on display.

They discovered they were going to be new parents, and Drake was about to be a big brother. Their son was born in August 1991, a beautiful boy with thick dark hair and brown eyes with long, thick eyelashes. Ejaz wanted to name his son after a great warrior. They settled on Jordan Ejaz Ahmad. His Muslim name was Tariq, signifying he belonged to the Islamic faith. Everyone in the family called him Jordan, but to Ejaz he was "Tariq." In Arabic, "Tariq" is the name of the morning star. Tariq was named after the Islamic general Tariq ibn Ziyad. This great warrior conquered Spain for the Umayyad Caliphate in the 8th century.

He grew to be a handsome boy; with big, brown eyes and dark hair he kept short and neat. Ejaz was very proud of his son, taking part in traditional Muslim practices as he grew. Jordan went to the Muslim Temple on Fridays, and then to Sunday school with his grandmother and mother on Sundays. He was taught manners from an early age, to respect others, to work hard, to be polite, and do his best always. "Dad-eee!" He would cry out to Ejaz, arms outstretched for a hug. "Dad-eee!" His vocabulary developed quickly.

The car braked suddenly, the occupants stared at the creature that was lying on the lawn next to the curb. As the creature sat upright, the driver gassed the car, shaking his head and laughing. Trick or treat!

Ejaz loved American traditions, and this meant Halloween was a time for both tricks and treats. He would don a scary mask to lie down on the lawn near the street. When a car approached, he would sit up, slowly, like a creature awakening, and stare at the car. Jordan and his family watched from the front window of Ernestine's home, and they burst out laughing every time. The expressions of the car occupants were always priceless, from shock to annoyance. Ejaz just laughed and laughed.

Summertime meant mowing the yard. While other people might groan and complain of the task, Ejaz jumped up and volunteered to mow at Ernestine's house. Ernestine's daughter, Johnny Joy, recalls how she looked outside to see how Ejaz had mowed intricate patterns in the thick grass. "What is he doing?!" she laughed.

"There's no grass where he's from," Ernestine reminded her with a shrug. "He just loves mowing." The two women watched him, giggling; his face read pure joy as he manipulated the mower to trim here, carve a path there.

July 4th meant Ejaz would come home with armloads of fireworks: sparklers, black cats, and bottle rockets. It seemed he always bought armloads of everything. He watched the colors of the sparks as they shot into the sky, the lights reflecting in his dark eyes. For Ejaz, the fireworks and fun represented his coming to the United States, fulfilling his mother's dream, and working hard to succeed. Still, there was so much to learn! The beauty of it all was that he *could* learn it; he was free to learn and grow. This was why; he would remind anyone who was listening, America was such a great country.

Ejaz purchased a video recorder, and he recorded scenes from his everyday life to share his experiences with his Pakistani relatives. He went to the mall with family and taped the indoor carousel, the food court, some of the stores. He videotaped relatives. Most of all, he videotaped little Jordan. "Look at this truck, dad-ee!" Jordan would exclaim, playing with a toy fire engine and showing its movable parts, lights, and sound. "Ah, very pret-ty!" Ejaz says from behind the camera, pride and mirth in his voice. He instructs Jordan to take a seat in a child-sized chair. "Tell me, Tariq, do you have a dream?" But the toddler was having none of it; the toy fire truck was far more interesting.

When he was six years old, Jordan accompanied his father to Pakistan. He gazed out the airplane window; the earth below looked like one big giant quilt. Stepping outside of the airport was like stepping into a fire; the thermometer read 106 degrees. They arrived in a crowded city that seemed, no matter where you turned, right on the edge of the sun. It was so far from Mississippi, and Jordan kept looking for green: trees, grass, plants, water. All he saw were brown hues atop more brown hues, with bright splashes of color from clothing and décor.

Jordan met elders, aunts, uncles, and more cousins than he could count during the six-week stay. Ejaz was so proud of him, and he took him to various sites and explained history, science, religion, and everything he could about the things they saw, the places they went. They ran on the beach and saddled up on a camel for a long, slow ride along the sand. Jordan excitedly reported their fun to his mom on regular phone calls, adding that he missed his family in the States. The experience was like an adventure story come to life, and in between were family members kissing and hugging and squeezing him in ongoing greetings. "It taught me that family is important," Jordan explains. "Even if they are thousands of miles away."

Ejaz always wanted the best for Jordan, but he did not spoil him. "America is a great country," he would remind his son, ruffling his dark hair. "You can be successful. I want you to be successful, and I want you to be happy."

Ejaz taught his son to play cricket, the most popular sport in Pakistan. He also took him golfing and swimming. Ejaz wanted his son to understand the value of work, so when he was old enough, Jordan would go to Regal Imports to work with his dad. He learned how to count money, run the register, and work with customers. He was a good salesman, politely answering questions, and talking about the items in the store. It was a delight to see the tall, handsome Ejaz softly instructing the cute, dark-haired boy how to run a store.

Ejaz kept a black backpack-type bag and it contained "important papers," he told others when asked. Friends assumed it had Jordan's information in it, such as birth and medical records. A close family member believes it was where Ejaz kept a large quantity of cash. Later, attorneys asserted that it was his immigration registration and other legal documents. At the time, however, no one thought to question the bag or its contents.

Later, it would have a role in a deadly game no one wanted to believe was playing out.

# CHAPTER 12

Ejaz loved his family very much, but there was one big problem: Bonnie had no interest in converting to the Muslim religion.

At first, it was just a subject to be debated, and then the subject became the source of squabbles, then arguments. "I want someone to worship with," Ejaz would explain.

"I go to the mosque with you!" she reminded him. Bonnie would wear the hijab when he asked; if they went to mosque or if his Muslim friends visited, she had no problem with wearing the hijab. "But I am a Christian," she told him. "If I converted to Islam, it would be a lie."

Bonnie was a spitfire, as they say in the south. She was unafraid to voice her opinion and she was fearless when it came to standing up to others if she felt wronged. While Ejaz respected this, he also needed her to convert to Islam, for religion was such a part of his life and world.

"I need my freedom," she was honest. "You know how, sometimes I tell you you're suffocating me, and I need to do some things on my own? Like, just go out shopping or whatever."

"But I am afraid something might hurt you. Someone will hurt you."

Bonnie would laugh. "You think they'd try?"

Things would calm down, and soon the argument would start again. Jordan was going to the mosque for worship. It was Ejaz's social outlet, and his life. Why could she not convert?

"Because it's not in my heart. Don't you want me to be honest?"

Soon, it became apparent that Bonnie converting to Islam was not going to happen. Bonnie was interested and respectful of Islam, she respected his beliefs, but she identified as Christian. And there again was that tiny voice in the back of her head, which mocked her.

*What if this is all a lie ... what if I'm only fooling myself...*

More arguments, more anger. Bonnie did not want to be tied down to anyone. She was feeling cloistered and claustrophobic. She did not want to convert to the Muslim religion because it would be a lie. It took some introspection, and Bonnie realized their connection to one another was now based on arguing. After the argument, they would make up with hugs and kisses, long talks, laughter. It was just like it was when they first met, until the arguing began again. She did not want their happiness to have to be fueled by arguments. She could not stand the cycle. She felt like her doubts had come true, after all.

Tearfully, she prepared to file for divorce. They had been together for seven years. A part of her was so heartbroken, because he was her soul mate. The practical side of Bonnie knew Ejaz would fight for custody of Jordan. "You should file on 'grounds of desertion,'" a friend advised. "That means faster divorce proceedings, and you get custody of your kid. And you don't have to pay an attorney a bunch of money. Money you don't have," she reminded Bonnie.

Trusting the advice, Bonnie cited grounds of desertion, believing that this meant she would be automatically granted full custody. "I lied," she would later admit; "I was young and stupid." Ejaz never hurt her, was never violent or abusive, she would later tell the courts.

Ejaz was in Pakistan when Bonnie filed. He was served just as he arrived home.

They began 1995 as single parents, splitting custody. Jordan went to live with Ejaz on certain weekends. Drake stayed with Bonnie. Bonnie could not bear to look into Ejaz's pained eyes.

Still, every chance he could, he begged her to return.

She refused, as painful as it was. Her freedom was that important to her. If they got back together, she knew the differences in religion would only tear them apart again, along with the feeling of being cloistered and the mistrust which had grown between them. Bonnie could not take yet another heartbreak.

Ejaz moved in with friends. He eventually purchased a red brick home located on a quiet suburban street named Sea Isle, in Memphis. He already owned several rental properties, but this home was being prepared for himself, Bonnie, and Jordan, should Bonnie return to his arms. Ejaz so wanted a happy family, all living together under one roof.

Jordan would get to spend weekends with his father, and when he was there it was customary for Bonnie to call their son and see how he was faring. Ejaz and Bonnie stayed on positive terms. Still, Ejaz pined for his one true love.

On August 31, 1997, Princess Diana died from wounds suffered in a car crash. It is estimated that three million mourners and onlookers lined the streets during her funeral, which was covered live, airing in two hundred countries. Ejaz was one of the 2.5 billion people watching the broadcast. "He cried like a baby," a family member recalled. "He just hit the floor and could not stop crying." But Ejaz was soon to fully realize the loss of another love, and his grief for this loss was even worse.

Bonnie was preparing to marry a man she had been seeing, Raymond Garrett. They had been sweethearts in their teenage years, and now Raymond had returned to her life. It was no clearer than ever that she was never going to return to Ejaz. Ejaz became so upset that he showed up at Ernestine's door. Neither Bonnie nor Ernestine had ever seen him like this.

"Please don't marry him!" He cried out when Bonnie came into the living room, holding Jordan's hand. "We still love each other!"

They began to squabble, with Bonnie trying to reason with him and Ejaz begging her back. Their words grew louder until Ejaz grabbed Jordan away from her to hug him tightly. "I have to be with our son!"

"No!" Bonnie yanked their son away. "Ejaz! You can come back and see him when you've calmed down!"

Something came over Ejaz and he stepped back. Fear and sadness washed over his face. Then he was angry. "I will take you to court to get the custody of my son!"

"That's it!" Bonnie snapped up the phone and dialed a number. Despite his never touching her, never hurting anyone, she filed assault charges against Ejaz.

When he left, a family member comforted Bonnie and Jordan, who were both crying. "You need to file charges against him," the family member told Bonnie. "A restraining order, in case he comes back."

"I can't!" Bonnie exclaimed.

"You have to," she was told.

Johnny Joy thought the whole thing was silly. Why take out a restraining order just because you were angry?[5] "Ejaz would *never* hurt anyone," she told her sister.

Heartbroken, Ejaz moved into the home on Sea Isle, alone, although he allowed friends to stay when they needed a place. Jordan was there on weekends, so he was not as lonely.

Raymond did not like Ejaz, because he knew how Ejaz had a place in Bonnie's heart that no other man could ever fill or replace. Bonnie knew this as well, but she tried to explain it in such a way that Raymond could understand. "There are different types of love," she told Raymond. Bonnie was still headstrong, and no one was going to tell her how to feel or what to do, so she continued being friends with Ejaz. Although Bonnie continued working with him on visitation for Jordan, Ejaz tried to stay away from Raymond.

One night, Ejaz came over to Raymond and Bonnie's home to pick Jordan up for the weekend. Ernestine was at the house. She invited Ejaz in. "Come on in," she told him. "Come see us."

---

5   Despite an extensive search, a record of this charge could not be located

Ejaz stayed outside. "No, I cannot," he told her. "It would be disrespectful to Bonnie and her husband for me to come into their home."

"Ejaz," Ernestine shook her head. "There's no problem."

"No," Ejaz shook his head. "I will not disrespect."

Ernestine knew how Ejaz felt about Bonnie and Ernestine confided that she believed "He still loved her. I don't think he ever got over her."

Still, Ejaz respected Bonnie, her new husband, and their children.

Today, Bonnie confides, "Sometimes I feel guilty ... I think, what if I hadn't filed for divorce? What if I had stayed with him?" Tears filled her eyes as her voice trembled. "If I had stayed married to him, he'd still be alive..."

# CHAPTER 13

In her fourth year of marriage to Raymond, Bonnie began to feel suffocated. She was not happy at home; she was not where she wanted to be. Raymond was using drugs and his life was spiraling out of control. One day, Ejaz showed up at her workplace to surprise her with some news. He was preparing to go to Pakistan and wanted to tell her goodbye in person.

What he found was a woman in tears, in emotional turmoil. He could not bear to see the people he loved crying.

She found herself telling him everything, and she could not bear to look him in the eye. Especially when he began to plead with her to come back to him.

Finally, Ejaz's shoulders slumped. Tears ran down his face. "Promise me," he made her look him in the eye. "Promise me, get yourself happy or leave him."

For days Bonnie walked around in a fog, trying to decide what to do. She loved Ejaz. She loved Raymond. She had to have the freedom to be able to make decisions for herself. Sometimes just hard work and limitations of marriage felt suffocating. She was raising children, working a full-time schedule, and trying to keep house.

One night, Raymond came in the door only long enough to get ready to go out again, and another fight broke out. In the middle of the shouting, Bonnie told him what she had learned only a few hours earlier. "I'm pregnant," she admitted.

Raymond broke down crying, slumping to the floor. "What do I need to do?"

The two had a long talk, and Raymond promised to become clean and sober, and he did. Both began to work hard to better the lives of their whole family. Raymond was sincere, and did what he needed to do to help.

When Ejaz returned to the States, Bonnie also had a long

talk with him. Ejaz was crushed. She tried to reason with him. "Raymond and I have a baby now."

Ejaz was wiping tears. "I do not care whose child it is. I still love you. Please come back!"

"Raymond's the father of my child," she told him.

His face bore more pain than ever. "So am I. So I was." Ejaz said, as he walked out of her world, leaving part of his heart behind.

He continued to be a huge part of Jordan's life. "He was an important teacher to me," Jordan says now. "Him, my mom, and my grandmother. My dad didn't just teach me how to act; he taught me how to live."

Ejaz remained close with Ernestine, who was his confidant and surrogate mother in many ways. He kept a nice home, decorating the house on Sea Isle with beautiful antiques, framed art, and knick-knacks and mementos from his home country. He remained an entrepreneur, working in various jobs and businesses.

Part of the Islamic faith requires a Muslim to help the community, to make the world a better place with charity. Ejaz, says family members, was the person to whom anyone needing help brought their problems to solve. Sometimes it was money, advice, a roof over their head, or a car to drive.

When Johnny Smith, Jr., needed a place to stay, Ejaz opened his home to his friend. Johnny slept on a mat in the spare bedroom. When he needed work, Ejaz hired Johnny to work in the fish market. "It was not a good job," Johnny says. "You could shower and scrub down, but you still smelled like fish!" Johnny worked alongside an African American man named Willie Jackson. Willie also did repairs on Ejaz's cars, but it seemed he did more damage than repair.

"Why do you let him 'fix' your cars, Ejaz?" Johnny demanded of his friend. "If you take it to him to fix, it's no telling when you'll get it back. He messes up everything he touches!"

Ejaz would only smile patiently. "He needs help," he

would say. "He needs work." Ejaz always had a driveway full of cars for Willie to repair at one of the homes he rented out where he kept nonworking vehicles parked. If Willie needed money, Ejaz never turned him down. Johnny only shook his head. He knew his friend never turned anyone away, but he also knew people like Willie would easily take advantage of such a situation.

Ejaz invited Johnny to meet Jordan. Sometimes Johnny accompanied them to take the ferry to Mud Island River Park, a favored landmark located on a peninsula on the Memphis side of the Mississippi River. A little over a mile from downtown Memphis, it features a river park, museum, amphitheater, and paved walkways to stroll along and watch the paddleboats, barges, and the flowing river. Sometimes Ejaz and Jordan would stand on the bank and just watch the river, enjoying the breezes and the sights.

One of Johnny's favorite stories is when Ejaz joked with everyone, saying, "If I die, John will not have any friends!" leading to laughter from the group.

Ejaz, and Johnny, had many friends. Ejaz's life was devoted to the Islamic faith, and he did not smoke or do any drugs ("Not even prescription," one of his closest friends remembers). None of his friends or family members can remember him ever even drinking alcohol. He was respectful towards everyone, including women, and he loved his son dearly.

When he met Leah Joy Ward, it seemed his life was perfect.

# CHAPTER 14

*I was already a prisoner while I was*
*free before I was locked up.*
*- Letter from Leah Joy Ward to Judge*
*Beasley, September 1, 2005*

The short, blonde woman stepped out of the nondescript vehicle and, without a backward glance, slammed the door and kept walking. Another john, another pocketful of money, and now on to her dealer to score. Such was the life of this addicted, street-wise woman Leah Joy Ward.

Perhaps the problems began long before December 16, 1976 when Leah was born in Ripley, Mississippi. Her mother delivered a healthy, eight pound ten ounce baby girl she named Leah Joy. The baby was the middle child of three children born into an upper middle class Pentecostal family. Leah's parents had been wed for over twenty years. Her mother obtained a college degree. Her father, a former military man, was a blue-collar worker in a local factory.

Like so many families, Leah's family had a history of substance abuse and mental illness. Her maternal grandmother was a recovering alcoholic and still used mild sedatives for her "nerves." She had aunts and an uncle who were also recovering alcoholics, and two of her paternal uncles had been hospitalized with a diagnosis of Paranoid Schizophrenia; one of the uncles was still hospitalized when he died. Leah's paternal grandfather was also an alcoholic.

As she grew, her hair turned strawberry blonde with a natural curl, and her eyes remained a pretty blue. Leah had no major upsets in her early years. When she was a little girl, she suffered an accidental fall resulting in a bloodied nose, which caused her to have nosebleeds during sinus problems for the rest of her life.

Elementary school presented no issues; little Leah loved school and her grades were always good. She got along with classmates and there were no problems reported by staff.

Things changed in fifth grade, where notes about her behavior began appearing on her progress reports. Leah had become sassy and smart-mouthed, talking back to teachers. Although her behavior was immature, she was physically maturing rather quickly. Leah later reported having admirers from the older grades. Teachers began picking up notes that Leah was busily scribbling instead of following along in class; notes in which she often wrote her sexual intentions to the receiver of her letter. At thirteen, Leah began keeping a journal of her sexual exploits detailing who she was with and what they did.

As she progressed through middle school, her grades were changing from A's and B's to D's and F's. Despite her declining grades, she was still promoted to the eighth grade, where she continued to attract older boys and mature young men.

On one occasion, teachers had to pull Leah and another girl apart as they resorted to angrily exchanging words and fisticuffs.

"She called me a slut!" Leah argued, seeing no reason why she shouldn't jump this brat and show her that Leah was not going to take this nonsense.

The name-calling and taunts were not limited to Leah's ears. Her brother was subjected to the rumors and innuendo about his sister as well. More than once he told his parents how tired he was of being told what a whore his sister Leah had become.

Besides the incident at school involving the fight, Leah had begun to act out against other authorities. She argued with an assistant principal about a reprimand she deemed unfair rather than take the punishment meted out. She was written up for the infraction. Rather than heed the lesson, she fumed that it was so unfair.

Leah's family had recently moved to a small town in Tennessee. They wanted a home where the children could play safely, and they found the perfect house surrounded by woods, a place where a kid could spend all day imagining and dreaming, safely out of the path of traffic. Leah played sports and was a good basketball player for the Adamsville Junior - Senior High School Cardinals, but not as good as her sister, who helped lead the team to State. As a kid she played soccer for the Blue Devils. "Devil," says a former classmate, was an appropriate name.

"She had a reputation for being wild," the classmate remembered. As Leah grew older, the "wild" went from simply sneaking out at night, to guzzling alcohol and taking hits of marijuana into the wee hours of morning. Her exasperated parents tried desperately to help her; they admitted her into local private hospitals because of her irrational, abusive behavior and substance abuse. Upon release from the hospitals, Leah would start out doing fine, obeying the rules and doing her schoolwork. Before long, it was back to routine, slipping out her bedroom window into the dark to find friends who had liquor or pot. She returned to actively disrespect others, and displayed a greater interest in sex and drugs than in family and school. She preferred the company of people who did not think she was on the fast track to hell just because she used curse words and wore makeup.

One family member wondered if it was Leah's strict Pentecostal upbringing that caused her to rebel so significantly. Some theorized that perhaps being told constantly that almost everything, except church, had the potential to send you straight to Hell; a teenager might just want to test the theory. Even better, if it upset your straight-laced parents.

Her parents were "good people," according to many, meaning there was no use of drugs or alcohol in the home. Law enforcement hadn't developed a "relationship" with the family due to constant police calls requiring their presence at the residence. They both worked hard at honest jobs to provide for their family who they cared about deeply. Having obtained her college degree, Leah's mother obtained employment as a teacher and her father continued steadfastly in his position as a blue-collar worker in factory work. In Leah's mind, church was a family anchor, and she had no use for anchors or anything else she believed would tie her down.

Leah's stint on the basketball courts was short-lived. She refused to do any homework and, when coaches asked, lied glibly about her schoolwork and assignments. Because of this and her faltering GPA, she was suspended. Leah found herself in the position of having to watch her team score points while she sat on the sidelines, again seething about how unfair life was, and not taking ownership of her negligent ways.

Her parents were appalled when Leah reported she had been date raped by a twenty-year-old black male. Charges were filed when the accused was in jail serving time for robbery. According to family members, the rape charge remained pending.

Leah's family asked themselves, "How much worse could it get?" They found out in March 1991, when the phone rang and law enforcement officials were on the other end.

An officer explained how they had responded to a call regarding a vehicular collision. Upon arrival, an adult woman was observed standing nervously beside a 1989 Cadillac. She reported that she was taking the car on a test drive, when suddenly a juvenile driver came roaring out of nowhere to smash into the Cadillac. When officers spoke to the juvenile, they discovered it was their daughter Leah; she was only fourteen years old. She stated that she was running away from home, and the car she was driving was her grandmother's, which she had taken without consent.

"Stolen vehicle" the report read.

Leah was also in possession of three blank stolen checks bearing her mother's name. Her family soon learned that Leah had cashed a fourth check for three hundred dollars.

Leah appeared in court, and was ordered by the judge to pay both the cost of towing for the Cadillac and repairs and the court costs, a total sum of $400.00.

It just seemed Leah was not willing to follow rules. Two months later, in May 1991, she was caught skipping school in order to meet an African American man at her home where they spent the day together.

The Department of Human Services was called out to the family home in early July of 1991 when Leah reported abuse at the hands of her father. She showed bruises on her legs which she reported were the result of being beaten with a switch. Leah said her father punished her by pushing and hitting her, shoving her into walls and slapping her. It was also reported that Leah had shoved her mother in anger. This time, it seemed Leah and her parents would get the help they needed when the family was ordered to attend counseling, and Leah was admitted into Lakeside Hospital a few weeks after the visit by DHS. Her behavior was out of control and she was deemed a danger to herself and others.

Once released from the hospital, a part of the treatment plan required Leah to be seen twice as an outpatient at the Lakeside Outreach Office in Jackson, Tennessee. They referred her to Quinco Mental Health Center. Quinco reported Leah "did not respond to therapy ... she [Leah] described the family sessions as only making matters worse."

Her family was at a loss as to what to do. Nothing had seemed to help. It grew increasingly frustrating and agonizing. Sometimes it seemed that their family's entire existence and efforts revolved around Leah Joy and her problems.

The day she stole her brother's truck, however, answered the question as to what to do with Leah.

# CHAPTER 15

Once again Leah and her father were exchanging words. The house rang with angry taunts and shouts.

"You have no respect for anyone!" her father thundered. "You don't even think before you act, you just do! Whatever rules we set, you have to do the exact opposite!"

Leah bolted out of the house, slamming the door behind her.

Her brother's truck was sitting in the driveway, key in the ignition. Leah squeezed behind the wheel, cranked the engine, and roared off. If she ran away, that would serve them right. She just had to get away from the houseful of people who just did not understand her. Later, when the cops called her parents, they had Leah in custody. Her brother's wrecked truck and a house trailer that was in transit to Savannah, Tennessee, before she had smashed into it, stood nearby.

Sometime between the release from Lakeside Hospital and wrecking her brother's truck, Leah tossed birth control methods out the window. It would serve her parents right, she fumed, if she did end up pregnant! She smiled, just thinking of the satisfaction she would get at their pious faces etched in horror and worry, an unwed teenage daughter in their nice, square, Pentecostal home. She continued breaking curfew, refusing to obey the rules in her home, and dove out of the bedroom window every chance she could, the moment the Tennessee skies darkened into night.

Leah's mother now had her daughter's promiscuity to worry about, not only that engaging in such activity might eventually catch up with her, causing her emotional harm, but also repercussions such as sexually transmitted diseases, or an unwanted pregnancy. She tried to talk to Leah about the potential dangers she caused herself, Leah just shrugged it off and continued to slip out of the house at night, to drink, party, and flirt. At their wit's end, Leah's parents filed an "unruly and runaway" petition. Her father signed the forms in an effort to help his middle child. Their out-of-control daughter was fourteen when she was admitted for an evaluation into the Timber Springs Adolescent Center located in Bolivar, Tennessee, in early September 1991.

"Why do you think you're here?" The intake specialist asked.

"Because of my father," Leah pouted. She appeared pleasant, the specialist noted. She was articulate and her neat attire was appropriate and clean. Looking beyond the big smile and sparkling blue eyes, the flawed judgment and the reasoning that was so amiss was quickly evident to others. Leah, however, seemed perplexed as to why a young teen, charged with, among other things, grand theft auto, and a history of substance abuse and violent behavior, would be in a treatment program.

Leah reported that she drank beer; sometimes vodka, and every now and then she'd sip on a wine cooler. Drug use was out of the question, she told them. She admitted how angry she was towards her father. She denied any sexual abuse, but reported physical abuse by her father. Leah had a "boyfriend" who was seventeen years old and African-American. As part of the program, she was put through a battery of testing, both educational and psychological.

Her achievement tests revealed her reading skills were in the twelfth percentile, her arithmetic in the fifty-fifth percentile. Her IQ was about 101, placing her in the average range.

The Reynolds Adolescent Depression Scale showed her to be within normal limits. She was not severely depressed, nor was she manic.

She was diagnosed as having an "Adjustment Disorder." The doctors explained to her that an "Adjustment Disorder" was a "stress related mental illness" caused by life changes and a person's inability to cope and adjust to those changes. As a result there can be serious consequences: feelings of being overwhelmed, making reckless decisions, anxiety, depression, and (sometimes) suicidal thoughts. Whether the changes in her life were positive or negative, Leah had not yet developed the skills to cope with them. Leah was prescribed mood stabilizers and mandated to attend individual and group psychotherapy. The social worker noted Leah did well in the therapy sessions, actively taking part and usually appearing to be happy and cheerful.

She was discharged from the Timber Springs Adolescent Center during the first week of October 1991, and was next moved into the Mercy Ministry Group Home in Monroe, Louisiana.

Leah remained in that program close to six months. She even celebrated her fifteenth birthday while at the group home. She seemed to do well in the program, participated in therapy, followed rules, and seemingly worked on her issues.

When she came home in May, it appeared Leah was finally on the right track.

Then the rebellious behaving began again: the talking back, the slipping out at night, the promiscuity, and the horrible displays of temper. One of her parents told officials that they were relieved that at least Leah had stopped stealing cars.

# CHAPTER 16

The family did agree that Leah could also be such a sweetheart. She could be so kind and gentle, sharing a good laugh and enjoying her life with others. During those moments, it was easy to enjoy her company. But when she was angry, it was just best to get out of the room.

As good as Leah's "sweet self" could be, her angry violent side was as bad. To them, it seemed as if she was possessed, screaming, eyes wild, face red, and throat pulsing. She was known to grab anything within reach and hurl it, or slam herself into her bedroom. They remembered a lot of slamming doors.

Afterwards, she cried and begged forgiveness. "I'm sorry, mommy," she would sniffle. "I didn't mean to break it, daddy."

"When Leah loses control, it seems she has the strength of five or more people," her mother later told authorities. The mood swings went from one extreme to the other; there was no middle ground.

Leah's mother continually wondered if Leah was using drugs or drinking, perhaps this would account for the horrific temper, the erratic mood swings. Leah tended to always hang out with the wrong type of people, thugs and n'er-do-wells, instead of people who loved their family, their church, and wanted to make something of themselves. Additionally, Leah could sleep for hours when she was at home, completely crashed out and snoring. If a jumbo jet made a takeoff in the front yard it could not have woken her; she could sleep through anything. Life was much quieter when she was in a slumber.

In October of 1993, Leah physically attacked her mother, slamming the older woman into a wall. It was the second time she had physically assaulted her mom, and the attacks were always frightening and painful. There is no record of this incident having been reported to law enforcement.

By now her brother had moved out of the house. He was the reliable child in the family, his parents later reported. He always pitched in around the house, was polite and hard working. Leah's sister, two years younger than her, still lived at home. According to Leah, she never had problems with her sister.

As an adult, Leah would self-report on her drug use to various agencies. She was not opposed to smoking pot on the weekends, using it as a chaser for the six-pack of beer she normally consumed. She enjoyed cigarettes, at least three a day, and burning through a pack a day on the weekends. She did not have an abuse problem with any of it, she told people. She just liked to party. She reasoned that it wasn't like she was doing it at home; to respect her parents, she kept the drugs and drinking away from home. She began taking Valium, Percocet, and Lortabs. Valium was her favorite, and she was downing at least five a day. At least she was not shooting up, she figured.

Drugs were so easy to get. Although her family still lived in a small, rural community, that didn't matter, drugs were plentiful. If you wanted them, and had the means to get them, you did not have to take the hour drive to Memphis.

When she was seventeen, Leah's behavior escalated to an even higher level of seriousness.

It happened on school property. One of her friends had a boyfriend, Victor. Leah had spent the previous day gobbling down valiums, and her mood again swung from smiling and friendly to erratic and uncontrollable. Victor and Leah began arguing loudly, and Victor shoved Leah to the floor. The humiliation was too much. Leah's famous temper came broiling to the surface. After she pushed herself up, she strode down the hall, shoving past sniggering onlookers, and out of the building. It was not long before Leah reappeared; this time she was holding a mean-looking knife. She leaped at Victor, the blade poised at him.

There was a skirmish and scuffling, and the knife was finally yanked out of her grip. Victor was unhurt. Leah was marched to the principal's offices. From there, she was escorted to the McNairy County Juvenile Court.

"I didn't want to kill him!" She insisted. "I wasn't going to kill him!"

"Then why did you do it?"

"That motherfucker made me look stupid," she seethed. "He was going to apologize for it!"

Officials tried to make her understand the consequences of her actions. They searched for remorse, or at least for an admission of guilt, in the young woman. They never found either.

"He shoved me first!"

The McNairy County Juvenile Court referred Leah back to Bolivar Timber Springs. It was her second appearance in court, and her third hospitalization. As a result of the incident, she was also expelled from school.

When the intake specialist asked her, "Do you know why you're here?" Leah gave a shrug. "I don't know."

Leah told them she had never been sexually abused, and sure, she was having sex, but she did not bother with birth control. Her brother now lived in another state, but her sister still lived at home and they got along fine. She liked basketball, softball, playing the piano, watching movies, and time with her friends.

Leah hoped, after leaving the hospital, she could just return to a normal life: school, friends, home. Her mother was concerned about whether or not Leah would even be allowed to return to school. Again, she prayed her daughter would finally learn there were consequences to bad behavior.

Leah was prescribed Prozac, and was told that she was going to be remaining at this center for a thirty-day visit.

The Psychiatric and Social Assessment read:

*Patient has a history of oppositional/defiant behavior ... she demonstrates a great deal of impulsivity in her behavior*

*... she seems to have little respect for authority or rules and regulations of society.... Patient seems to feel, at this point and time, that she should be allowed to do as she pleases.*

Leah was subjected to personality testing, to include the House-Tree-Person Drawing Test (HTP) and the Millon Adolescent Personality Inventory (MAPI). Her drawings indicated she had problems including impulsiveness, aggression, self-depreciation, and low self-esteem (though not suicidal), and was in denial of problems.

The MAPI results indicated:
- Histrionic and aggressive behavior
- Low level of empathy for others
- Self-defeating behaviors and feelings of being misunderstood and unappreciated
- Impulsive and volatile displays of anger caused by intense conflict between the need for dependency and self-autonomy
- Restless, erratic, and highly offended by trifles
- Unhappy with her physical appearance

Leah was diagnosed as having a Conduct Disorder, "Solitary Aggressive Type" with an alcohol and drug abuse problem. She had a developmental reading disorder and "features" of a Borderline Personality Disorder. The "Axis IV – Severity of Psychosocial Stressors" was at level 4, considered severe, and her triggers were listed as the legal charges against her, the unsuccessful hospitalizations, and the conflicts with her parents. The recommendations arising out of her psychological evaluations included:

*Leah needs a long-term alcohol and drug abuse treatment in a secure, structured inpatient facility, where she can also receive counseling with a focus on anger management and improvement of prosocial behaviors.*

Later in life she would be diagnosed as bipolar. According to the National Institute of Mental Health, bipolar disorder is a brain disorder; it causes noticeable shifts in a person's mood. Bipolar is not the normal "highs and lows" of life. In the "manic" phase, the person has a period of a "high," where multitasking is easy, the energy level is high, they need little sleep, they are gregarious and funny, but keeping a train of thought is difficult, as if the brain "jumps" from one idea to the next. When in a manic phase, the individual displays behaviors of risk-taking and impulsivity, such as shopping for multiple unnecessary items, imbibing a dangerous level of drugs and alcohol. The "depressive" phase is the opposite: severe depression, exhaustion, very little ability to concentrate, and even suicidal ideations.

During each hospitalization, Leah denied any form of sexual abuse. That declaration eventually changed, but because of her penchant to lie and exaggerate in efforts to manipulate others, its veracity was questionable. Leah always seemed to know what buttons to push to get her way.

She did tell officials that her father was abusive in his punishments and in his anger. He had shoved her into walls, hit her with a "switch," had slapped and punched her hard enough to cause bruising. She explained that it made her want to rebel against him, and disobey at the slightest order or request. Any little thing he said to her would anger her.

The medications stopped when she was released from the hospital; Leah tossed the Prozac out.

At seventeen years of age, Leah Joy had bounced around from hospital to hospital, appeared in juvenile court twice for serious infractions, and was known as a thief, liar, and manipulator. Her family, though trying to be supportive, clashed continually with Leah's ill-conceived notions of what she should and should not be allowed to do. School fared no better, as it also made demands that she follow the rules and laws, which she detested. A substance abuser and sexually promiscuous since she became a teenager, Leah seemed to be out-of-control and on a very dangerous path.

Then she married.

# CHAPTER 17

Larry Ward was born and raised in Adamsville, Tennessee, and his family attended church at the same church as Leah and her family. For a while, Larry considered Leah's brother his best friend. His sister was Leah's good friend. The girls had sleepovers at one another's houses where they spent time talking and giggling. Larry only knew Leah as his sister's little red- haired friend, and never thought of her as much more, until a chance meeting changed it all.

It was in 1994, just another day at the Ward house, when Larry's sister, with Leah in tow, came in through the back door. Larry was dating a pretty blonde girl and had no interest in meeting anyone else. Leah sat down on the couch nearby and they started talking.

Larry's dry wit made her giggle, and Leah's pretty face and polite conversation interested Larry. He admired that she was a talented artist; she could look over a picture just once then sketch it to perfection. They began seeing more of one another.

Then, Larry explains, "We got to monkeying around."

When Leah announced she was pregnant, Larry was flabbergasted. Up to this point he had never thought about being a father, much less an actual hands-on dad. He examined his feelings carefully. In his heart, Larry knew he was not crazy, head-over-heels about her, but he did love her.

Larry's cousin, Winston Munroe, recalls pulling Larry to the side. "Don't do it, bro," he told Larry. "She's trouble. You're getting yourself into a mess."

"She's pregnant," Larry insisted. "I want to do the right thing."

Winston was already biting his lower lip and shaking his head dramatically. "I'm warning you. It's going to be bad. You know she's been locked up in the loony bin? And she still stays in trouble."

Larry was insistent. He was going to be a father, and it was important to do it right. "Besides," he told friends and family, "in a lot of ways she can have a real good heart." He asserted that Leah just needed a chance, someone to trust her and take care of her. "I believe anyone who has kids should get married, should work, and love each other," he argued. Later, he found himself repeating, "I have the worst luck in picking women."

Leah's version was that they married because her parents forced her into a loveless marriage. She reports Larry was abusive, to the point that one beating forced her to flee for help to a local hospital. Larry adamantly denies the accusations.

Larry and Leah became Mr. and Mrs. Ward, saying their vows before a minister in the minister's office of Loving Truth Church. Leah's parents and Larry's sister and her husband were witnesses.

The newlyweds set up house in a rented trailer on the outskirts of Adamsville. As soon as they set the "welcome" mat on the porch, even as the last box was unpacked, Larry felt as if he had made the biggest mistake in his life.

She was moody, and her mood swings would fly wildly from one extreme to the other. She could be a sweetie, cooing to him in that slow, soft drawl. Minutes later, it seemed, she was shrieking at him, throwing things in every direction.

Three days into the marriage, Larry was flying down a back road in his truck, ruminating over his new life. The windows were down, the stereo blaring. The wind filled his ears with a roar and ruffled his short brown hair as he considered everything transpiring.

It appeared that his new wife did not want to be a wife. He had a feeling she was still using drugs. He never knew if he was coming home to the sweet Leah he had first met, or the evil woman whose job it seemed was to make his life hell on earth. They had a child on the way, but...

With one deft movement, Larry pulled off his wedding

ring and flung it out the window. He did not watch it land, bouncing through the dirt, to settle into the weeds.

# CHAPTER 18

In March of 1995, Leah felt the first stabs of labor pain and was rushed to a hospital in Selmer, Tennessee. She was in labor for four hours, intermittently gasping and crying out in pain. Leah gave birth to a nine pound baby boy she named Christopher.

Marriage did not seem to settle Leah, nor did being a mother seem to change her for the good.

Later, she reported to administrators in a psychiatric ward that for a "few months" in 1995 she was using both cocaine and meth.

One evening, when Larry was showering, Leah burst through the bathroom door. Larry, trying to rinse the soap out of his eyes, was blinking against the steam and water. He realized Leah was standing in the bathroom, a kitchen knife in one hand and a carving knife in the other.

"I'm going to kill you, motherfucker," she seethed.

Swallowing the fear, he dared not move. "Girl," he told her slowly, "You might get one stab in, but I promise you, I'll have you on the floor in a minute."

Later he would recall, "It was crazy. It just got crazy."

He described how he often woke up in the morning and reached for her, only to realize her side of the bed was cold and the bedroom window was open. Larry took care of Christopher, bathing, dressing and feeding his son. He did nothing about Leah, because he knew she would come slumping through the door in a few days, as was her pattern, asking forgiveness and swearing she was going to change.

Whereas, once upon a time, she had shared secrets with him, now she was keeping secrets from him. She had earlier confided in him that when she was thirteen years old, an African American man raped her. Larry says he later found this alleged rapist was a part of Leah's current social circle, even after he had supposedly sexually assaulted her as a young girl. He wondered why, if young Leah was raped by this man, she would hang out with the accused as an adult.

In July 1996, after a five-hour labor, Leah gave birth in a hospital in Selmer, Tennessee, to a daughter Sallie, who weighed seven pounds. Sallie was a pretty little girl who would grow to favor her mother. They eventually moved into a small apartment closer to town to accommodate the growing family.

Maybe now, Larry hoped, maybe now Leah would settle down. Leah seemed to adore Sallie. He felt Christopher was being pushed aside and Sallie was her mother's favorite.

Still, Larry says, he tried. He is the first to admit he was not perfect. He smoked weed and snuck alcohol in his youth. He made enough mistakes. But he did love those kids, and he still felt for Leah. "I just keep trying," he would say.

The one thing he swears he did not do is that: he never physically hurt Leah. He never slapped, shoved, kicked, or punched her. Several family members readily agreed that, Larry is not the type of man who would hit a woman. He was wiry, muscular from hauling and lifting on the boat. He could have a temper, but it took time to build. Sure, he cussed her out enough times during fights. He was strong enough to have sent her flying with one punch. But it was never in his nature.

There was one incident, however, when Larry was almost ready to break that steadfastness pattern.

It was time to leave for Memphis to catch the tug at Mud Island. Larry told about how he gave his children long hugs and kisses on their foreheads. He hugged and kissed Leah goodbye, telling them all again how much he loved them and would miss them. Still, Christopher was crying mightily for Larry.

Leah's father and Larry's cousin, Winston, waited by the car to drive him to Memphis, a little over an hour's drive away. They both witnessed what happened next, Winston explains, and to this day it angers him.

Little Christopher was standing inside the front door, his hands against the screen. His crying was tearing Larry's heart out. "It's okay," Larry kept telling him. "Daddy will be back soon. Don't cry!"

Leah walked to stand behind little Christopher and she swung the screen door open. Larry stopped, thinking she was going to allow Christopher to run outside for one more kiss and hug. Instead, Leah put her foot against the little boy's back and shoved him so that he landed sprawling on the pavement.

It was so surreal that, at first, no one could speak or move. Christopher's wails turned into cries of pain at his skinned knees and hands.

Winston's beefy hands were closed into fists as he growled at Larry, "If you don't kill her, I will." It snapped Larry back from the surreal moment, and he took off running after Leah.

As Winston was scooping up Christopher and trying to brush the blood and grit from his little hands, Larry was racing after Leah, who ran screaming out the back door. Just as Larry was returning to gather his little boy in his arms, a Selmer City Police Department cruiser pulled into the yard.

As Larry was being handcuffed, he demanded to know why he was the one being arrested. Couldn't the officer see the scrapes on the crying toddler?

"Domestic violence," the officer told him. "Your wife done called you in."

Leah loved to take photographs, and she would often take five to ten pictures of the kids in the same pose. She dressed them up in the cutest clothes and snapped away, calling out in a gentle voice to look into the camera. "But that was about it," Larry explained. "She loved to take their pictures," he said, describing the extent of her motherly activities.

Friends and family began questioning their relationship. Larry told them, "She's mean. Mean, and a cheater."

"Then leave!"

"She's the mother of my kids," he would always say. "She's my wife."

He still cared about her, and, at times, even was able to enjoy her company. Leah had a good sense of humor. She had talents, like her artwork, and she did seem to care about people, to some degree. She sometimes displayed a loving side to her nature. When Leah wanted to be, she was the perfect partner.

On the outside, it appeared their life together was blissful: a pretty little girl, a handsome little boy. Larry still had his "country boy" looks, lanky with close-cropped hair, and Leah was pretty, with her bleached blonde hair. For all appearances, they seemed to fit well together. Few people knew how her life spiraled out of control, where one drug led to another, one shot glass led to a bottle. Leah no longer had the ability to stop, but admitted only that she considered herself as just dabbling in meth and cocaine, still enjoying a good toke of marijuana.

One of Meth's street names is ice, because it resembles small chunks of frozen water; the formal name is crystal methamphetamine. Meth was also called "crank." It can be smoked in glass pipes, injected, or inserted in a body cavity for a high. Users can feel the high for up to twelve hours as the drug's effects rush into the brain's neurotransmitters. After the crash, it's back to the dealer who obtained the stuff from a "meth lab," where the crank is manufactured in a complicated process in a cavernous room, or on a kitchen stove using the right utensils. Some industrious "cookers" will mix it in a bottle while being driven around in a car to avoid detection. The stench is akin to cat urine or rotten eggs. It is dangerous when cooked. Plenty of abandoned mobile homes dot the Tennessee rural landscape, the kitchen side blown to bits from a meth operation gone badly.

"Crack" cocaine is the poor man's cocaine, and it looks like small, cream-colored rocks. It is cocaine in solid form, a mixture of the coca plant with baking soda and water.

Despite the use of baking soda to "thin out" the cocaine, it is a highly concentrated drug, far more addictive and lethal. The dramatic increase of dopamine, norepinephrine and serotonin makes for a fast, euphoric high. Leah Ward had discovered what all users discover: no high is as good as the first, which lasts less than 20 minutes, so the user chases that elusive first high, always seeking it; though they will never find it, thus one hit is never enough. Leah found herself in that endless pursuit.

Once the body has its first taste of a street drug, it is difficult to stop the cells, organs, chemicals, and nerves from needing that rush. In order to chase that high, a person has to have money. There are fast ways to make immediate money. Prostitution, topless dancing, and drug dealing are the easiest ways women in the lower socioeconomic classes know how to accumulate that fast money. Leah was no exception.

Larry's phone rang with a call from someone else who lived in the same apartment complex that Leah and Larry Ward called "home." The caller asked Larry if he was busy.

"What's going on?" Larry asked, momentarily stopping work.

"Larry, you got to get those kids out of that apartment. When you're gone, she's bringing in all kinds of no-counts. You do *not* want your kids around these people."

When Larry hung up the phone he rubbed his hand across his face. How many times was he going to get calls about what Leah was doing when he was away from home?

According to many people, Leah had quite the houseful when Larry was gone to work. They went in and out at all times both day and night. Cars parked and were gone within minutes. Anyone going in or out either kept his or her head ducked down, or strutted around looking for a fight. Christopher and Sallie were growing up in the chaos, right in the middle of it all.

Larry had a job he loved and it paid good money. He worked on one of the tugboats that pushed the barges up and down the Mississippi river. He was gone from home for a while, and then would return home on leave. "Heaven is right there on the Mississippi, up near Knoxville," he promised. "No houses or freeways, nothing but trees and the river." He was well respected on the boat, and he learned which captains were best to sail under and who to stay clear from.

He wished his home life could mirror the river life: peaceful, welcoming, and tranquil. It was not to be.

BAM BAM BAM BAM!

Larry Ward jumped in his chair. The pounding seemed like it was going to come through the apartment door. The kids looked up from playing. Leah, however, remained in the back room. BAM BAM BAM BAM!

Larry peeped out the window to their front porch. It was night, but by the tiny porch light he could see the biggest, blackest man he had ever encountered.

Larry slowly opened the door, ensuring the security chain remained hooked. "Look here," he tried to sound brave through the crack in the door, "I have a gun in here, and I have my kids in here."

His unwanted visitor was rooted to the spot. "I don't give a damn about your gun or your kids," his voice was a baritone. "I just want my fuckin' money." He made sure Larry was listening. "The bitch done stole from me one last time. I'm not leaving 'til I see her."

The door closed, the safety chain rattled, and Larry swung the door open. "She's back there," he pointed. Then he scooted the kids into another room and considered his gun.

By then, the barrel-chested man was rumbling down the hall. Larry followed. He watched the man yank Leah as if she were made of rags. His entire hand wrapped around her arm in a tight grip. Larry wondered if it would snap the bone.

He shook her like she was weightless. "You bitch!" Another hard shake. "YOU DON'T ROB ME!"

Leah was whimpering and crying. "I'll get it to you! I'll

get it to you! I promise!"

"You done stole from the wrong man, bitch! Where's my fuckin' money?"

She cried out in pain. The more she pulled away, the harder he gripped. "I promise! I'll get you the money!"

He dropped her to the floor, turned on his wide heel, and walked out the door, ignoring everyone else. The door shut quietly behind him.

Larry stood there in disgust, staring at Leah lying on the floor and nursing her arm.

"Larry," she finally whispered, "Can you loan me money to…"

Larry shook his head, not knowing if he should laugh or cry. Then he told her what he had been telling her all along: "I'm not giving you money for drugs."

In February of 1999, Leah got a job as a CNA in a Selmer nursing home. The job lasted until December. She then worked for a time at Murray Lawnmowers. Employment was not constant. Work, like parenthood and marriage, did not consistently appear to be in her plans.

They eventually moved to Crump, Tennessee, hoping to start over. Larry still desperately wanted the marriage to work for the sake of his kids. He kept hoping Leah would start to change, see what she was doing with her life. She was so pretty and smart, and could be such a wonderful person at times. He felt people could get off drugs if they tried. Larry admits he was no angel, and he had his youthful crazy times, but adulthood had settled him. So maybe Leah would settle down, too, and things could be normal. Sometimes it did seem like she was dedicated to a happy home life.

Just when he thought things were better, he would come home from another stint on the tugboat and open the door to a dirty house, piles of filthy dishes, and the babies in full diapers. Cleaning up behind her, he would tell her exactly what he thought of her. It seemed to work, and then out the bedroom window she went after the rest of them had fallen asleep. She would be gone for days, while Larry took care of Christopher and Sallie. "I had to be the momma and the daddy," he reports. "And I'm not saying I was ever perfect, because I'm not. I was never perfect. But I love my kids."

They fought over the filthy house, the neglect of the kids. "What am I supposed to do?" Leah raged. "You're never around when I need you. You're always gone to work!"

Larry says he quit one job in an effort to appease her, to be home more often with his family.

"How could you quit?" Leah chastised him for weeks. "That was good money! You had security!"

Larry loves cars. He loves classics, hot rods, and motorcycles. He raced motorcycles for a short time, and he enjoyed riding his bikes and tinkering around with them. When Leah "borrowed" his Mazda RX-7 without asking, he swore that was the last straw.

The last time he saw her in his RX-7, she was driving and an African American female he did not recognize was in the passenger seat. The car was found on the side of the road, stinking from crack cocaine. Larry had to have the car professionally cleaned to get the stench out of the carpets and seats. Upon inspection, he discovered someone had removed a clip from inside the steering column and inserted a bread tie. He never knew why.

Later, he was told his car had been used in a string of convenience store robberies. Leah just laughed at the last bit of information, thinking it funny that Larry was a suspect in serious crimes.

Larry Ward says he lost all respect for Leah after she kicked Christopher, but he left for good after he came home from the boat to find a group of strangers in his house. They were there talking to Leah about Sallie's adoption, he was told. This time it was not surreal; he showed them the door quickly.

Leah moved out, leaving her kids with Larry. One of Larry's family members moved in. "She went black," he remembers. "She only started dating black guys. Or foreigners."

Larry discovered Leah had filed a restraining order against him. Afterwards, she had called him to chat. He told her he wanted nothing to do with her drama. It was not too long after he hung up that a police cruiser was pulling up and an officer was knocking on his door. He found himself under arrest for violating an order of protection filed on April 21, 1997. "Me!" Larry guffawed. He showed the officer the phone's caller I.D. "*She* called *me*!" No arrest was made, and the restraining order was dismissed.

# CHAPTER 19

Like many drug dealers, MacArthur Borner says he, himself, never used drugs. He even refused an aspirin if he had a headache. Nonetheless, he found the business of selling drugs quite lucrative, a way to make quick money in Selmer, Tennessee, a town of about four thousand, where the median household income is fifty percent lower than the national average, and the unemployment rate hovered at around sixteen percent. There is money to be made in dealing drugs in a town where the median income for African American persons, like himself, hovers at about $12,000 annually.

Selmer is a town that squats right in the middle of hundreds of acres of cotton fields. Long, sporadic remnants of the white fluff line the main highway until approaching Adamsville. There is only one Selmer newspaper; it has been doling out the latest information since 1902. About eighty-five percent of the residents are white, and there is an almost visible line between "black neighborhoods" and "white neighborhoods."

MacArthur Borner was only one of the players in the McNairy County underground world whose pockets are lined with cash from ill-gotten gains. Usually gregarious, he could become intimidating with those who owed him that money. He stood close to six feet tall, with a large girth and thick limbs. His skin had darkened from doing work as a truck mechanic under the hot Southern sun.

McNairy County's biggest claim to fame is Buford Pusser who served as Sheriff from 1964 to 1970. Pusser lived in Adamsville but operated out of the county seat of Selmer. His story was lionized in the 1973 movie "Walking Tall." The home of the former no-nonsense Sheriff is now a museum. The area boasts a ballpark dedicated to him, a street has been renamed "Pusser," and there is an annual Buford Pusser Festival. Sheriff Pusser is a renowned symbol of law enforcement taking down illegal activities, the main illegal enterprise in his time being stills that pumped out homemade liquor.

Illegal liquor is no longer the biggest crime problem in the area. Criminals flock to small towns and rural areas because the country affords isolation; a smaller law enforcement department means less police and fewer sophisticated crime fighting measures. The latter is important for people like MacArthur Borner.

On this particular day in April 1999, MacArthur strolled up to a business that was a popular meeting spot and drop-off. The business owner, Lance Tuck, was involved in shady dealings. MacArthur recognized his regulars, skinny, nervous girls who would do anything to get a taste of cocaine or crack. This time there was a stranger, a pretty girl, with them.

They all made small talk while money and drugs changed hands. MacArthur listened to the girls as they talked to the blonde, who said her name was Leah. MacArthur then realized who she was; they had family members who worked together at a local company.

"Hey," one of the girls told her, "you'd get a lot better blow if you went with Sal, and if you fuck him, you'd get it for free." They erupted in a burst of giggles.

MacArthur recognized the name "Sal" as a local dealer, his competition. Leah seemed to be considering the thought.

"What are you doing, here, girl?" MacArthur asked her. He nodded at the stringy, yipping women. "You're too nice a girl to be hanging out with them girls."

Leah said she bought the cocaine, using the euphemism "blow," and shared it with her friends.

"Them ain't your friends," he advised her. He looked at her closely. MacArthur was quite familiar with the signs of addiction; he saw it in the majority of his clientele. He saw it in Leah now. "Don't use your body just to get high," he told her. "You're a pretty girl."

They talked some more. She shared with MacArthur that she had broken up with her husband, and had two little kids, sometimes spending weekends with them. Leah left with MacArthur Borner, who tells how he was determined to get her clean and sober. She moved into his house but never moved into his bed. They remained just friends. MacArthur says now he ensured he did not do business with Leah around, and Leah spent time recuperating. For the six months that they lived together, Leah stayed clean, according to MacArthur.

She worked part-time as a CNA at a long-term home health care center, making $6.50 an hour feeding, showering, and changing the linens of long-term patients. She helped to comfort them in dark times, offering chitchat and laughter to make things sunny. Her supervisors would later say she had a good future in this type of work. She self reported working there from February 1999 to December 1999. Her reason for leaving was "moving to Memphis."

She was pretty, with red-blonde hair and sparking blue eyes. She was witty, fun to be around, and she had a genuine niceness to her. "A real sweet girl," MacArthur recalled, years later. There was nothing bad about Leah herself; she was just addicted to a drug that could make her go crazy. And when Leah went crazy...

MacArthur recalls a time when one of her acquaintances, someone she had shared dope with, said or did something that made her angry. MacArthur does not recall what was said or done, but he certainly recalls Leah's reaction. She seemed to become another person, screaming, ranting, and cursing. "If she woulda had something, she woulda used it," MacArthur says now. Luckily there was no available weapon, and the argument was forgotten.

Leah's temper was legendary among those who knew her. Well-mannered and smiling one moment, she could burst into anger the next. "She could be mean," a friend says now, "it doesn't matter who it was made her mad – her mom, her kids – if someone pissed her off, she was mean. She could be downright evil."

# CHAPTER 20

Lance Tuck needed a favor from MacArthur Borner, and Leah Ward agreed to go along with the plan. It would result in Leah's first time as an adult to be placed in handcuffs.

It was only twenty days into the new year of 2000, and Lance's business remained a popular meeting spot as well as a place to buy and drop-off drugs. Lance asked MacArthur to go pick up his van and a quantity of illegal drugs, then meet Lance back at the business with the goods. They determined a place in the business where the drugs would be secreted for clandestine pickup.

MacArthur and Leah had no problems picking up the van and the drugs. With Leah in the front seat, smoking a cigarette and making small talk, MacArthur rolled up to the café and parked the van. The drugs were placed, and MacArthur and Leah returned to the van.

"POLICE! FREEZE! POLICE!" They just appeared seemingly out of nowhere, officers with guns drawn and grim faces. Both MacArthur and Leah were placed against the car and searched, then handcuffed. A small amount of marijuana was found on Leah.

MacArthur was no stranger to this game. He had already spent time in prison. He understood, in the business of drug dealing, you took chances. Sometimes it was being in the wrong place or at the wrong time. Sometimes, as in this case, MacArthur felt it was a snitch.

Snitching was not in MacArthur Borner's criminal code, so he refused to answer questions or say anything to incriminate anyone. He wondered what Leah was doing in the other room when they interrogated her, but he knew she was solid; the girl was not a snitch. As he envisioned, Leah said nothing to law enforcement that they could use.

"I'll get you an attorney! I'll help you out!" Lance Tuck promised. MacArthur turned down the offer and obtained his own legal counsel. He knew Lance was blowing smoke, and suspected Lance of snitching him out.

Bonds were set and MacArthur and Leah consulted with their separate legal counsel. Leah's bond was $20,000, and she need only to pay ten percent to be released. MacArthur knew a man in Gulfport, Mississippi who would give them honest work while they waited for trial, he explained to authorities. They would go down to Gulfport, work for a living, and then return for the trial. It was agreed.

MacArthur had spent most of his life working on trucks, to include engine repair and driving. He worked loading and unloading the big trucks at his friend's business. Leah was hired by the same man to clean houses. They remained friends, and their boss allowed them both to share his own home. It was a simple life. They worked hard all day, and then came home to relax, where often MacArthur would pull out a checkerboard or chessboard, and Leah would watch them play.

They tried to explain the nature of the game to her. "This is the rook, see," MacArthur showed her. It can only move like this," he slid the piece across the board. "Or like this." He moved it again, sideways.

"Uh huh," she nodded.

She tried the game, and although the men assured her she had a good grasp of the rules, she determined chess was not her forte. She would rather play checkers. Sometimes they watched television together. One thing MacArthur notes of their stay in Gulfport: Leah never used, nor voiced any interest in, drugs. The five months spent in Gulfport was free of any illegal activity, according to MacArthur Borner.

The indictment for Leah and MacArthur was filed mid-2000 and an arrest warrant was issued. Leah and MacArthur were booked into the Harrison County Jail ten days later.

"Then the feds caught our charge, and brought us to Jackson," MacArthur explains. The U.S. Marshalls arrived to take custody of both Leah and MacArthur.

After consulting with their attorneys, Macarthur and Leah decided pleading guilty was in their best interest. As a result, the sentence was reduced. They both went before a Judge in the Federal Building in Jackson, Tennessee to formally plead.

On November 13, 2000, Leah received twenty-seven months with probation. For the first time, Leah Joy Ward was going to prison. It was MacArthur's second charge, so he received 188 months. MacArthur was shackled and his transfer to prison began. He never saw Leah Ward again … until she made the newspapers for a much more serious crime.

# CHAPTER 21

In January 2001, Leah Joy Ward became inmate number 06103-043, transferred to the Federal Prison Camp (FPC) Bryan, located in Texas. Almost a hundred miles northwest of Houston, the minimum-security prison offers far more freedoms than a medium or maximum facility, but it is still a prison, restricting an inmate's movements and their overall lifestyle. The prison has a system where seasoned inmates assist and introduce new inmates to the facility with a tour and introductions. Leah's "tour guide" explained the women could order food, beauty items, sundries, and limited medical supplies from the prison store, called a "commissary." While purchases were limited (soups limited to 12, shampoo limited to one), inmates may purchase an approved number of clothing, such as sweat suits, T-shirts, and athletic sneakers. Leah settled down to life behind the high fences, one of about nine hundred incarcerated women who were doing their time.

The federal inmate uniform remained prison-issued tan pullover shirts and pants. As with all prisons, the opportunity to better oneself is there with educational classes and training programs, therapy appointments and group therapy. As on the outside, a person must truly want help before they will make the commitment to change. Leah began attending A&D (Alcohol & Drugs) treatment several times a week. She was prescribed Trazodone as well as several other medications.

At a later date, Leah was transferred to Federal Prison Institute (FCI) in Tallahassee, Florida. While the security level remains low, it is one step higher than a FPC on the federal prison security scale.

According to Leah's self report on a job application, she began employment on January 2001 at a Memphis City School via a "temporary job placement agency." Her position was in data entry, where she proofread school lunch forms, then typed the information into a computer. She made $7.50 an hour. She worked until November 2001.

Christopher and Sallie were five and four respectively by September 11, 2001, while their mother was completing her sentence in the federal prison. September 11 was like any other morning until television news interrupted with graphic images of American Airlines Flight 11 and United Airlines Flight 175 flying into the twin towers of the New York World Trade Center. At the same time, American Airlines Flight 77 crashed into the Pentagon. United Airlines Flight 93 was heading for the White House when passengers attempted to overthrow the hijacking terrorists, causing the plane to crash into a Pennsylvania field. Almost 3,000 were killed with at least 6,000 others wounded. It was discovered a group of Islamic al-Qaeda terrorists were responsible for the attacks. The result was an invasion of Afghanistan, the creation of Homeland Security, changes in anti-terrorism legislation and law enforcement powers, enhanced security procedures in airports and public places, and much discrimination against anyone from the Middle East or of the Islamic faith. For so many across the United States, "Muslim" became synonymous with "terrorist." For a time, it seemed like the world was coming to an end; many people made preparations as the sales of water, gas masks, and guns peaked. It was a time of bafflement and fear across the country, from major cities like Los Angeles to tiny hamlets like Adamsville, where Larry Ward continued to live with his children.

Larry Ward was not shocked when he learned Leah had been arrested, tried, and convicted for a drug charge along with her codefendant, a thirty-six-year-old African American male named Macarthur Borner. After all, Leah was involved with some dangerous people, and he assumed that since she had "gone black," Borner must have been her lover.

For many people in McNairy County, a population of fewer than 27,000 people, for someone to date or marry a person of another race was unacceptable. Once again, Leah was bucking a system. First drugs, then her black friends, and now this, folks shook their heads. What was next?

Leah was released on parole in October 2001. She would be twenty-one years old in a few months. She was given an apartment in a Memphis halfway house, set up with the assistance of an organization dedicated to helping parolees get on their feet. The organization began assisting her in job searches; she received aid for food and necessities.

It was only four months, after all. Rules were simple: no drugs or alcohol, unannounced drug testing, curfews, find a job … easy enough, everyone around her agreed.

A few months after her release, she tossed the medications that would balance her brain chemistry, adjust her moods. She later reported a family physician was prescribing different types of medication for her, including antidepressants and sleep aids.

Leah started the new year of 2002 working for a Kmart store in Memphis. She made $7.75 an hour waiting on customers, stocking shelves, and ringing up purchases on the cash register in the jewelry department. She was gregarious and pretty, assisting shoppers with their items.

Larry began talking to her again, and he brought the kids to her apartment at the halfway house. He swam with the kids in the community pool and spent time with Leah, allowing her to see her children. They were her kids, Larry reasoned, and she had a right to see them. Besides, they were still legally man and wife.

Leah quit her job at Kmart in November 2002. She cited "attending school" as her reason for leaving.

The summer quickly turned to fall. The unpredictable Tennessee weather, when temperatures dip low enough to cause a freeze; creates dangerous "black ice" on the roadways. Memphis was no exception. The truckers who steered their rigs up and down nearby I40 will affirm: black ice is most dangerous. It can sneak right up on a driver if they don't pay close attention.

That year, black ice was not the only danger that snuck up as unforeseen through Memphis.

# CHAPTER 22

Looking back, Ejaz's family recalls, September 2002 was a time of bitterness. The day of the terrorist attack, now called "9/11," continued to send ripples of dissent throughout the world as the first anniversary of the attacks was marked. Strangers glared at Ejaz Ahmad and his friends from the Middle East; they lumped all Muslims together as terrorists. Ejaz felt travel was too unpredictable. It did not feel safe for him and his law-abiding Muslim friends. He sadly made the decision to not travel home to Pakistan until the climate settled.

Besides the discrimination, September 2002 is marked as the beginning of the long, hard fall from which Ejaz's loved ones would never recover.

Regal Imports was now closed because of the rise in crime in the mall. Several businesses had been robbed and lack of safety and security caused many stores to close down or change locations. Ejaz had closed his store the previous year. He sold some of the furniture to his friend, Walid Salam. Eventually the mall would be demolished.

Ejaz was at home when his mechanic, Willie Jackson, showed up at Ejaz's home on Sea Isle with a pretty blonde girl in tow. "She don't have no place to live," he told Ejaz. "She needs help, somewhere to go. She's sleeping on the street and don't have nothing to eat."

Ejaz merely stared at Willie. "I cannot live in the same home as a woman not my wife," he said. "It is against my religion!"

The girl came into the room and made small talk. She introduced herself as Leah, and said she was having a rough time. She wanted to be a nurse and better herself. She just needed someone who believed in her.

Ejaz lamented. He felt bad for the girl. Her dark hair had been bleached a pretty blonde, and it hung just past her shoulders in long, graceful, natural waves. Her sea-blue eyes lit up when she talked. Her bright smile revealed a small gap between her front teeth. She was smaller than Ejaz, standing just a little over five feet tall, but she was built sturdily. She could hold her own in conversation, and she was sweet-natured.

She seemed sincere and harmless.

Ejaz listened, as she explained in her slow, Southern drawl how she had nowhere to go. He felt bad for her. He offered her a house, rent free, until she got on her feet. It so happened that one of his rental properties was open, he explained. It was not in a great neighborhood, but it would be shelter.

As she listened to Ejaz, Leah's eyes traveled over his nice home; a one-story red brick with white trim and black shutters. A big tree lifted upward and spread its branches over the front yard. The inside was decorated attractively, with thick couches and patterned wallpaper. The window treatments were gorgeous. Ejaz, among many things, was a talented decorator. It was not a stately home, perhaps a thousand square feet. There was a small kitchen, a large bonus room converted from a garage, a nice-sized living room, three bedrooms and one bathroom. One closet was full of handmade rugs, antiques, and items brought over from Pakistan. A beautiful, expensive Pakistani rug covered the floor. A sliding glass door led to a back patio. There was a backyard enclosed by a privacy fence, with a metal shed in the far corner of the yard. It was a middle-income neighborhood, nothing fancy but definitely nicer than the cinderblock walls and barbed wire she had recently called home.

Leah did not bother to tell Ejaz that part of her story.

"We cannot live here together," he told her. "It is against my faith. I am Muslim."

Leah nodded, seemingly expressing understanding. She was, she told him, very interested and respectful of all cultures. She was divorced, she said, with two children who stayed with their maternal grandmother. It was partly true; she was still legally married to Larry Ward – another detail she preferred to leave out of their conversation. Larry maintained that he was the one raising Christopher and Sallie all along.

"You was living with somebody before," Willie told him.

Yes, Ejaz explained, but that houseguest was a man, a friend of his who needed a place to stay. The older houseguest was a roommate until he returned to Jordan, bidding Ejaz thank you and goodbye. But it was against his faith to live with a woman who was not his bride or his family. They discussed the numerous rental properties Ejaz was managing.

Leah moved into one of the rental properties, but Ejaz fretted over the neighborhood. He felt bad for putting this woman, single and alone, in such an area of town. The crime rate in Memphis was on a steady upward trend. This was one of the reasons Bonnie never wanted to move to Memphis, Bonnie had always told him.

After some debate, Ejaz notified Leah. "I am going to get you out of that house," he told her. "I do not want you to live where you are not safe."

Ejaz told her she could live in this house. He would go stay with a friend. So as Leah was moving into the Sea Isle home, Ejaz was moving out.

The fact that she had a safe place to sleep and a loyal supporter was great, but she needed money to buy the illegal drugs her body was now craving and demanding. She hit the street, making fast cash the easiest way she knew how. She dressed up in what Ernestine Marsh would later call "hooker clothes." Her hidden life was another john, another pocketful of money, go to her dealer, and score.

Larry recalls that Leah still maintained her halfway house's apartment in Memphis. He was again a full-time parent to Christopher and Sallie. Leah would come take the kids for occasional visits, then head for Ejaz's house. Larry was aware she was seeing a man from some other country, but he knew nothing else. "Once I'm through, I through," he says of relationships. He had given all he could, and his friends and family had been relieved he had finally understood that Leah was not going to change. He wanted nothing to do with her unless it was about their children.

Sometimes Larry felt like he was bungling through parenthood. He made them do their homework, mind their manners, and hoped he was doing the best. He dated occasionally but mainly focused on the kids.

With Ejaz's encouragement and money, Leah started school, attending classes in between work. She enrolled in the Patient Care Assistant program (PCA) at Concorde Career College in October 2002. She made good grades, the letter "B" appearing regularly as her GPA. Ejaz happily paid her tuition, encouraging her. A college education is so important, he would tell her.

Leah would later explain to Jordan why she had such a seemingly crazy schedule. "I'm a nurse's aide," she told him. "That's why I have to be out all night, and sleep all day." She worked as a Certified Nursing Assistant, or CNA. CNA's are not medical assistants; they assist with patients by taking blood pressure, temperature, and helping patients with hygienic care. CNA's provide care to aging patients. They complete health surveys or private patient information. Leah was employed at a hospital; she also did home health care. From there, she attended classes. Every workday, she packed her satchel with her scrubs and a few necessities, slung it over her shoulder, and headed for work, a photo ID tag swinging from a pocket.

It was later discovered by Ejaz's friends and family that she sometimes left "for school" but was making a detour to a friend's house with one goal: to get high. Instead of books, pens, and papers in her school bag, she carried Ejaz's things to pawn or sell.

Despite this hectic schedule, sometimes she invited her

kids to stay at the house with her. Later, she cared for Jordan when he visited, along with Christopher and Sallie. Her children didn't ever stay long. They were quiet and followed the rules, sweet kids, but always returned to Selmer.

When Ernestine Marsh met Leah Ward; she wondered just what Ejaz had gotten himself into.

Ernestine first met Leah when Ernestine made a rare visit to the house on Sea Island.

Ernestine was entering the house behind a happy, grinning Jordan, who was excited to be staying this weekend with his dad. As she came in through the front door, Ernestine saw a blonde-haired woman asleep on the couch. Jordan breezed past the living room; it was evident he had met her. Ernestine thought it strange that Ejaz would have some woman slumbering on his couch.

The woman stirred, and she was sitting up as Ejaz came into the room. He was wiping his hands on a kitchen towel, and Ernestine could smell the exotic spices cooking in the kitchen. "This is Leah Ward," he said as the blonde stretched, blinked sleepily, and then stood for formal introductions. Her hands were feminine, with tapered nails; Ernestine could see they had been professionally manicured. She was dressed simply and had a wide smile, showing a gap between her front teeth. She had pretty blue eyes. Leah's voice was soft and almost a monotone.

Immediately Ernestine detected an issue. This woman would look everywhere except in her eyes. Even as she was being introduced, Leah averted her eyes from Ernestine's face.

Ernestine followed Ejaz back to the kitchen and Leah sunk back into the couch. "She is tired," Ejaz said as he lifted a lid from a pot on the stove. A delicious smell bubbled out as he stirred. "She had to work all night last night."

"What are you doing? Why is she here?"

He shrugged, replaced the lid on the pot. "I am helping her out," he told her.

"Ejaz! This is your home!"

He smiled at her, his dimple showing. "Now, I am just visiting. I am not living here! She needs help, a place to be. I am helping her go to school."

Ernestine made herself stop talking. He may be a grown man, and legally divorced from her daughter, but Ejaz was still her son in many ways. Ernestine was immediately unimpressed with this Leah woman. And she knew Ejaz would always love Bonnie.

On her way out, Ernestine told Leah, "Glad to meet you! I hope you do well in school."

Leah smiled, but averted her eyes again.

*Maybe she's just shy,* Ernestine told herself as she took the path to her car. *Stop acting like a cop. You're no longer in that business.* Still ...she knew something was amiss.

# CHAPTER 23

*Wives, submit to your own husbands, as to the Lord.
For the husband is the head of the wife even as Christ
is the head of the church, his body, and is himself its
Savior. Now as the church submits to Christ, so also
wives should submit in everything to their husbands.*
*Ephesians 5:22-33*

*And among His Signs is this, that he created for
you mates from among yourselves, that you may
dwell in tranquility with them, and He has put
love and mercy between your [hearts]...*
*The Quran 30:21, on marriage*

Ejaz and Leah talked. "The only way we can live together is if we are married," he told her. "Perhaps we can become closer? People learn to love another."

Perhaps it was for all practical reasons. Perhaps it was sincere. A close friend to Ejaz explained, "I think he felt sorry for her. And I think he wanted to be married, to have someone there with him so he wouldn't be alone." Ejaz was lonely, said the friend, and he felt Leah needed someone to protect her and believe in her.

As in any culture, a Muslim wedding encompasses tradition. Family and friends gather. The bride and groom show and celebrate their love for one another. A family is planned for the future. In some cultures, marriages are arranged for young people, and their dates are chaperoned.

The diversity and commitment to tradition depends on the man and woman's level of piety. They may elect to include all traditions, or only a few.

Ejaz still lived with friends before the wedding. Although they were to be married, it was still improper for him to live under the same roof with a female that was not his wife. He did occasionally visit to help her.

One October day in 2002, Jordan was in school at his desk when he received a note to go to the principal's office. He shouldered his book bag, tucked his pencil into his notebook, and headed down the hall, anxious. *Why does the principal need to see me? What did I do?*

Instead of the principal, Ejaz and Johnny Smith, Jr., were waiting in the office. Ejaz was grinning and Johnny smiled and waved to Jordan.

"Dad! What – why did you get me out of class? Is everything all right?"

Johnny could not stand the mystery. "You're dad's getting married to Leah!" he blurted out. "We checked you outta class so you could go!"

Jordan considered it, but then he sighed and told Ejaz, "Daddy, I can't. There's testing going on and I can't miss it."

Ejaz's grin disappeared, but he nodded. "Go to class and take that test," he told his son.

"Are you sure? You're not mad?"

Ejaz gave him a tight hug. "Tariq, you must do well in school."

Jordan walked back down the hall. Part of him felt badly for not attending. He liked Leah. If she bought something for her children, she would buy something for Jordan. When her kids came to visit, he was invited to join them in everything they did. She treated him like family.

At the time, it seemed wonderful. Later, Jordan wondered if her behavior was just another game.

Leah Joy Ward exchanged vows with Ejaz Ahmad at a mosque in Memphis on October 5, 2002. Professor Kafait Malik performed the ceremony. Johnny Smith, Jr., acted as witness. Among the guests was Ejaz's friend Naseer Meer. Neither Johnny nor Naseer had met the bride until this day.

It was a lovely ceremony. Ejaz looked very handsome. His eyes sparkled with happiness; it was evident he was excited about having someone to grow old with, to raise a family and live in peace.

Leah was physically present, but observers would later report she did not appear to be emotionally or mentally available.

Johnny watched Leah. He noted Leah was not smiling, and deep down she seemed saddened, even depressed. Whatever was going on, the girl was not happy to be a bride. *"Something is wrong with her,"* Johnny told himself. *"I can see it in her eyes."* Ejaz, however, seemed so happy and settled. Now he had someone to share his life.

Ejaz moved back in to his home on Sea Isle with his new bride.

Unknown to Ejaz or any of his family and friends, the marriage was a sham. Leah had never divorced her first husband, Larry Ward.

*Salah* ("Connection") is the Islamic regular prayer that occurs five times daily for those over nine years of age. Clothing must be clean and cover the body to represent modesty. For women, donning a hijab is necessary for it represents that while she is judged on outward appearances, Allah recognizes her for her actions and heart. Allah loves her for her soul and not her charms.

The hijab is a veil or scarf that covers the head and chest of Muslim women, donned at the onset of puberty and worn in the presence of men who are not the family members. It is also a word that may refer to the seclusion of women from men in public, or it refers to another dimension, the veil that separates the world from God, *"Al-hijab."* Mostly, it represents privacy and modesty. "And when you ask [his wives] for something, ask them from behind a partition. That is pure to your hearts and their hearts" (Sura 33:53). Veiling is part of history, as far back as 2500 BCE. The elite wore them for respect and as a sign of high status. Greek women of high society were expected to cover themselves with loose-fitted clothing. The veiling is not only found in the Qur'an, but in the Bible as well. It is mentioned, for example, in both Isaiah and Genesis.

The hijab to some, both Islamic and non-Islamic, is a symbol of purity, morals, and modesty. Others view it as a control mechanism by men. Some feel it is a way to reject western cultures and mores. Some governments have enforced the wearing of cover, while others have banned the practice.

Thus the hijab can mean many different things to different people.

To Leah it was a sign of dominance. Her headful of pretty, thick blonde hair was hidden under a plain scarf, and it seemed restricting, like a vise, as if she was now bound to a man. Still, photos show her smiling brightly while wearing the hijab. Her dress became much more conservative, and she no longer smoked in public; instead, she puffed on her cigarettes at home in the back yard. She even eschewed makeup.

Some wondered if Leah's wearing the hijab was another jab at her families' religious values, a passive-aggressive way to keep angering or shocking her parents.

A close friend of both Ejaz and Leah observed she only kept the scarf over her head long enough to take part in traditional practice. As soon as she could, she pulled it off and shucked it away.

# CHAPTER 24

The first time that Bonnie knew a woman named Leah Ward existed, it came as a total surprise. She can recall, years later, the details of meeting her ex-husband's new bride.

Ejaz parked his car in the driveway and walked up to Ernestine Marsh's house to pick up Jordan for the weekend. Bonnie was there with her mother, and they both lit up when they saw him. As Jordan ran to pack, Ejaz told Bonnie, "I want you to meet my wife."

Bonnie merely stared at him, then stepped outside. It was cold, and she pulled her coat closer around her body as she walked over to the passenger's side of the car. It was no joke; a blonde haired woman sat in the front seat of Ejaz's Cadillac. *No shit*, Bonnie told herself. It *is* true.

The woman sitting in the passenger's seat had already rolled the window down. She was pretty, and she was watching Bonnie carefully as Ejaz's ex-wife walked up to the car. Before she had a chance to introduce herself, Leah slowly extended her hand out of the window.

Bonnie went to shake hands, but Leah's handshake was limp. She slowly dragged her nails across Bonnie's palm as she retrieved her hand. "Hiiiii," Leah said in her slow drawl as the tips of her fingernails gently creased Bonnie's palm. "It's nice to meet you." Her voice was slow, almost as if she was bored with everything around her. She certainly was the polar opposite of Ejaz. Bonnie could feel it, see it, and even taste the blonde woman's instant, angry, raw jealousy. Leah did *not* like Bonnie.

One thought instantly went through Bonnie's mind: *You're a vicious, conniving snake.*

Both of the women read one another so easily, Bonnie from what she deemed her "second sense," and Leah with the street sense of a criminal and a former inmate. They eyed one another with mistrust.

When Bonnie returned to the house, her face was a study. "That," she finally told Raymond, "was weird."

"What happened?" He asked her.

Bonnie looked down at the palm of her hand where Leah had drug her nails. She was shaking. "That woman...Ray, I felt it. She's evil."

Later, she and Ernestine compared notes. "Mom," Bonnie said somberly, "Something is wrong with that woman. When I shook her hand, I could feel it. She was polite, but her hand was ice cold."

Bonnie also confided in her best friend. "You mark my words," she was angry. "She's going to take him for everything he has."

Seven months later, Bonnie's premonitions came true.

# CHAPTER 25

"Leah's behavior was paradoxical," Ejaz's friend Kafait Malik later explained to investigators. She "was obsessed with Ejaz, but would disappear without explanation."

Walid Salam remained friends with Ejaz. Like Ejaz, Walid ran several businesses. Walid was a partner in a mechanic's shop and car lot called Vance Avenue, located on Memphis' Vance Street. Ejaz had brought a few cars to Vance Avenue for repairs. One of those times he brought Leah along, but Walid was not in the shop, so they never met, at least not formally. He met her at a time when introductions were not a good idea.

Walid, his female secretary, and Ejaz were enjoying lunch at a chain restaurant called Spaghetti Factory. They were laughing and talking over their pasta and salads, enjoying time off from work.

Out of nowhere, it seemed, a blonde-haired woman came storming up, demanding to know who the secretary was and why Ejaz was with her. She was furious. An embarrassed Ejaz excused himself from the table and walked off with the fuming woman, who continued to throw hateful, snarling glares at the secretary.

This was Walid's first encounter with Ejaz's wife, Leah.

Ejaz explained over and over to Leah that the woman was Walid's secretary, and they were just enjoying an Italian meal together. "She is Walid's employee!" He insisted. "I do not see other women!"

Ejaz returned to the table as Leah stormed off. He was embarrassed and apologized to his lunch companions. Walid did not understand Leah's anger; it was a simple lunch between friends. He knew Ejaz respected marriage and would never cheat. He politely changed the subject and they continued to eat.

It would not be the last time Walid heard Leah Ward's

name.

That Thanksgiving, Ejaz joined Leah's family for the traditional feast. Larry arrived and the kids ran through the house giving hugs and kisses. The smell of turkey, dressing, and baked goods filled the home. Larry avoided being near Leah. As usual, Leah was snapping pictures of Christopher and Sallie. Larry and Ejaz had little chance to interact, but Larry watched Ejaz. He saw him as pleasant, easy to get along with. He wondered why Ejaz had not seen through Leah's ruse.

Ejaz eventually wandered over to Larry while Leah was momentarily out of the room.

He smiled and extended his hand and Larry shook it. Ejaz said in his clipped accent, "I hear you are mean."

Larry snorted and looked over in Leah's direction. "Buddy, you don't know 'mean.'"

# CHAPTER 26

I LOVE YOU. It was written in red lipstick across the glass top of Ejaz's table. It was a message from Leah. She could be so sweet and loving. And then...

Looking back, there were so many signs, "red flags" that at the time meant nothing; they were just little things here and there.

True to his faith, his friends and family recall, Ejaz did not cheat on Leah or have sex with other women. It was very important to him that he remained faithful to Leah now that she was his wife, even when he found out she was stealing from him.

Ejaz noted Leah had withdrawn a thousand dollars out of his account without notifying him, without even mentioning it. When he asked her, she told him she had purchased Christmas gifts for her children. "A thousand dollars!" he confided to Johnny. "For gifts? You know she does not need that much money for a few gifts."

It did seem like a lot of money to buy gifts for children she rarely paid attention to. It was not money Ejaz could easily afford to lose, and the way she went about it, withdrawing the money without telling him, was suspicious.

She admitted to him she was on medication for bipolar disorder, formerly known as manic-depression. Bipolar disorder can be treated with medication to control the mood swings, but the person must take their medication exactly as described. Leah was not one to stick to a schedule for medication.

When Leah's two children visited, they got along well with Jordan. They seemed to enjoy their time with their mother. But something they said had bothered Ejaz, made him question his judgment, made him doubt Leah's honesty.

"Why did you marry my mommy?" they asked in their innocence. "Mommy is married to our daddy."

Ernestine later recalled a comment that Leah's mother had made to Ernestine when the two families had a brief chance to meet. At the time, it didn't have any meaning for her, no more than an observation shared. "Leah," her mother confided to Ernestine, "has a temper like her daddy." Later it would all make sense.

Ejaz loved animals, and he decided to keep chickens in the backyard. When they started to cover the back porch with droppings, was when he decided the chickens had to go. "Ejaz kept a very clean house," a close friend remembers. "He didn't like the poop near his house." Jordan was allowed to keep one of the chickens as a pet. The speckled bird had a nest in the storage shed where she laid her eggs. The hen was not as messy as a flock, and Jordan adored the bird. The next creature to inhabit the yard was a goat.

A neighbor gave Ejaz an old dog kennel and this became the goat's home when the temperatures dropped. Ejaz's friend Johnny just shook his head. A goat! But it made his friend happy, and it was a clean animal. At least, initially.

Ejaz, Johnny, and Leah were on the back porch when the goat ambled up to stand on the concrete. It sniffed the air, flicked its tail, and then dumped a load of pellets onto the immaculate patio.

Johnny burst out laughing. Ejaz screamed. He grabbed the first thing available, a screwdriver, and chased after the goat, shouting. Johnny was doubled over. Then a strange thing happened.

Ejaz hurled the screwdriver at the goat, meaning to hit it in the backside. Just as the goat turned, the screwdriver tip hit it in the heart. The goat fell over dead.

Johnny's mouth was open, but he was no longer in hysterics. The two men stared at the goat, then at one another. "You couldn't ever do that again if you tried!" Johnny marveled.

Ejaz was pale. "I did not mean to do it!"

They conferred. Ejaz was a practical man. He knew what

they did with a dead goat in his home country, and he knew how good they tasted.

Johnny remembers Ejaz slaughtering the goat. He also will never forget Leah's reaction. He can hear her words today, and they give him chills.

Leah was incensed. "How would you like it?" She shouted at Ejaz, "If someone cut your throat and then chopped off your head!"

# CHAPTER 27

Ejaz again noted some strange activity on his bank account. He spoke to Johnny Smith, Jr., about it. "She took money out of my account," he told Johnny. "This is not the first time."

"I know," Johnny told him. "I remember when you told me."

"What should I do?" Ejaz asked. "Should I tell her to leave? Should I tell her to get out of my house?"

Johnny sighed. "You have to do what's in your heart," he told his best friend. "Do what's in your heart."

Johnny knew Leah would physically strike out at Ejaz. He believes Ejaz would never hit a woman, or anyone else for that matter. If he was fighting for his life, or protecting his family, particularly Jordan, Ejaz would fight. He could be hotheaded and shout at someone who made him angry, but Ejaz was, overall, said Johnny, a nice man who, because of religion and personal values, would never hit a female.

Johnny doubted Ejaz would ever even use the gun he kept in the house.

When he had purchased the gun, Ejaz had told Johnny, "I need this gun to protect my home."

Johnny looked at the gun. It was a black automatic. Ejaz had owned the gun for a long time, and Johnny secretly wondered if it would even fire, because the bullets were old. Prior to Jordan's visits, Ejaz wrapped the gun up in cloth and stored it in the back room, on a high shelf that not even Johnny could reach. He carefully hid the gun so Jordan would never find it. Ejaz did not want an accidental shooting. Neither of the men considered Leah bothering with the gun.

When Johnny would visit, he often stayed for a few months at a time with his best friend and new bride. Ejaz again gave him a job. Their work was often interrupted by Leah's phone calls.

"Where are you?" She talked so loud anyone standing near Ejaz could hear her. "Are you with some girl?"

"No!" Ejaz insisted. "I am at work with John."

"You liar! I know you're with some other woman!"

"I am not!"

"Liar!" she shrieked.

The men exchanged looks. Johnny just shook his head.

Johnny Smith recalled a typical dispute between Ejaz and Leah. He was staying with the couple and, on this weekend, Jordan was visiting his dad. Leah became angry at the fact that Bonnie called Jordan to check on him and see how he was enjoying his visit. In a fit of anger, Leah tried to yank the phone out of Ejaz's hand. "Why do you let her call this house?!" She shrieked. "She has no right to call here!"

"Tariq is her son," Ejaz tried to explain. "She has the right to speak with her son."

Leah was fuming. "Are you seeing her?" She demanded. "Are you with her when you leave this house?" Then she stormed out of the house. "I'm out of here!"

Ejaz went after her, trying to talk to her. Johnny watched from the window as Leah began hitting Ejaz, screaming at him. She swung at him, shoving him. Ejaz's hands went up to ward off her blows. He kept trying to explain. Johnny could hear it all the way in the living room.

Ejaz came back in with a mark under his eye that was already swelling. "She hit me!" Ejaz told his friend in disbelief. "Johnny, tell her I do not do that! I do not – I would not – be with another woman! I am not such a man. I am married!"

Johnny went outside to console Leah. She was still fuming. "Ejaz ain't seeing another woman," he tried to calm her down. "Ejaz can't mess with another woman 'cause of his religion. And anyway," he told her, "Even if he could, he wouldn't do it."

"He makes me so angry," Leah grumbled, "I could just kill him!"

At the time, it meant nothing, just angry words from an angry woman. Besides, Leah's outbursts were becoming the norm in the Ahmad household.

Johnny Smith lost contact with Ejaz when Johnny went to Fort Lauderdale, Florida, for Christmas 2002. He moved in with a family member for some time. While there, he had a dream that haunts him to this date.

*He dreamed he was watching Ejaz and Jordan standing on a riverbank overlooking a large river, just as they did when they visited Mud Island and stared out at the Mississippi. As he stepped closer to join them, Johnny felt shock and fear. The water was gone from the river, and all that was left was muck and mud in an empty riverbed. Suddenly, the shoreline where Ejaz stood began to turn a deep color.*

*As far as he could see, the riverbed had turned to a deep red color which had begun leaking out of the earth. Johnny watched as the riverbed filled with blood.*

# CHAPTER 28

Leah seemed to get along with everyone else. She was never abusive towards any of Ejaz's friends. She could be polite, even sweet. Jordan liked spending time with her. But when it came to Ejaz, particularly if she was not taking her medication, it seemed all the teeth and claws came out.

Johnny Joy, Bonnie's older sister, was so busy with her children and work she rarely saw her mother and siblings.

Ernestine discussed an incident that Ejaz shared with her. Leah took Jordan, Christopher, and Sallie to the shopping mall. As they walked through the mall entrance, Leah gave them instructions. "You can go look around," she explained, "but be back in one hour. I'll meet you right in this spot." So she left three children, all under the age of ten years old, to walk the cavernous mall alone.

The kids looked at toys and gazed into the store windows, then eventually became bored. They headed back early to the spot where Leah had designated as a place to meet. As they walked up to her, Jordan heard Leah on her cell phone talking to Ejaz. "I don't know where they are!" she was telling him. "I told them to be back here in one hour. One hour! You're going to have to do something about this!" Jordan watched her, puzzled, as she hung up the phone. "When your father gets home," she warned him, "he's going to take care of you!"

Ejaz telephoned Ernestine in a fury. "She left them alone!" He raged. "Little ones, alone, in a big mall!"

A close friend of Ejaz's says Ejaz never looked at other women. He could be flirtatious, still a sharp salesman, but once he had the ring on his finger that was it, not even an appreciative look at a pretty girl. And despite her behavior, he was very protective of Leah when he feared for her safety.

Leah continued to work as a home health care aid, working a shift staying at a client's home as their caregiver.

She began making bizarre phone calls to Ejaz when she stayed with a male patient. "I don't know what to do!" She whispered breathlessly. "This man's flirting with me; he won't leave me alone!" She whimpered, "I'm so scared he's going to rape me!"

Destiny Reyes, Call Coordinator for the Health Care Company that employed Leah, received a call around midnight. It was February 1, 2003, and the call came from Leah Ward, who was sitting with a patient, Ms. Stout, at the client's home. "Ms. Stout's mother and sister left me alone here with Ms. Stout," Leah told Destiny. "Ms. Stout's father is here with us. I don't feel right with him here, and just me!"

"Did something happen to make you feel uncomfortable?"

"No."

"Well," Destiny advised, "give them a few more minutes to get back there. They should be back soon. Let me know right away if anything happens to make you feel uncomfortable."

Leah agreed and they both hung up. Not five minutes after Leah's call, Destiny Reyes received another call.

It was Ejaz Ahmad on the other line. Destiny was unsure if he was Leah's husband or boyfriend; he told Destiny to contact Leah immediately. "Something is wrong with her phone!" He sounded worried.

Frowning, Destiny dialed Leah's cell number. Leah answered, but due to a poor connection they could not understand each other.

The next call came just after their forced disconnection. Ms. Stout's mother was on the line. "We're home now," she told Destiny. They chatted just a few seconds.

Destiny logged the next call at 12:17 a.m. Ejaz was calling, and he chastised the coordinator for leaving Leah alone with a bad man in the home. "It is not professional!" He told Destiny in his clipped accent. "It is dangerous!"

"Sir, that's not what happened," Destiny told him. "She was not left alone in any danger."

Ejaz would not be placated. "I am going to look at federal laws," he told the coordinator, still angered. "I want to see if this is legal!" He was extremely irate, insistent that Leah was left in peril.

Destiny Reyes braced for another strange call, and sure enough it came at about thirty minutes after hanging up with Ejaz.

The caller was the client, Ms. Stout's mother. She was both irritated and worried. "Our caregiver's boyfriend called," she reported. "He says Ms. Ward has to come home right away ... some sort of emergency?"

*Good grief.* Destiny rubbed her eyes. She had the woman put Leah on the phone. "Leah," Destiny's voice traveled over the wire, "we don't have anyone to take your spot right now."

"But ..."

"If you leave your client alone, you *will* be reported to the state for abandonment."

Chastised, Leah hung up.

Destiny Reyes' phone rang again some fifteen minutes later. Ejaz was on the line, raging. "Leah has been left alone with some lunatic man!" He was shouting, yet sounded truly frightened. "This is not professional! Let me speak with your supervisor!"

"Sir, I am the supervisor on call." Destiny tried to soothe him. "I understand your concern for safety, I do, but this is not the case at all. By law, I can't give you much information. I can tell you, she is not alone in a house with anyone dangerous."

Destiny Reyes thought the problem was solved, and she was ready to file the incident report, until the following day.

Ms. Stout's mother spoke with Destiny at length. Destiny learned Ejaz had been waiting outside the Stout home, when the mother and sister had returned from their errand. "He cursed at me, and said he wanted to know why Ms. Ward was left alone with a strange man."

"What happened next?" Destiny Reyes was taking notes.

"I just said, 'it won't happen again,' and went inside the house. You know, we had to finally just turn our phone off, because he would not stop calling."

On February 3, Leah was called into the office. She was given a reprimand for "Conduct/Behavior." Leah was told she could have endangered the clients if she did not follow policy and procedure relating to her family and friends. Her behavior, she was told, disrupted her assigned duties and certainly gave the home health care company a bad name. She was placed on a thirty day probation. Her next review was scheduled for March 3, 2003.

Later, when vying for an appeal in her criminal defense case, Leah obtained a copy of the incident report and added it as an exhibit to her request for appeal in an attempt to show just how "dangerous" Ejaz was, a loose cannon with a hair-trigger temper. She labeled it "Employer Incident Report on Ejaz Ahmad."

Leah graduated with a degree in the PCA program on April 8, 2003. Ejaz, who had paid her tuition, was proud of her for following her dreams. His pride and her degree did nothing to heal the chasm that had grown between them, courtesy of Leah's lies and deceptions.

# CHAPTER 29

By now, the neighbors on Sea Isle were used to the sounds of bickering coming from within the walls of the Ahmad house. Neighbors had their spousal riffs. It really wasn't anyone's business. Anyway, it never lasted long.

A family member witnessed a horrible argument.

"Where were you?" Ejaz had demanded of Leah. "You never came home! You were out all night!"

"It's my job!" She spat. "I'm a nurse's aide!"

"No! You were not at work!" He thundered.

"The hell I wasn't!" She shouted back, just as loudly.

"I have a right to know! Where were you?" Ejaz raised his voice in frustration. "You were out all night! You did not call me! I did not know where you were!"

"It's none of your fucking business!" she screeched.

Ejaz often telephoned Bonnie to talk about Jordan. He confided in Bonnie still, despite their divorce and his marriage to Leah. And Leah was now the main topic of Ejaz's conversations. He was both angered and saddened by Leah's behavior.

"If she does not change," Ejaz vowed, "I will make her go. This house, this house belongs to Tariq and me! I will never give it to her."

"I don't blame you," Bonnie agreed. "You are paying for it, and it is in your name."

"Bonnie," he sighed. "I do not want to fail at marriage. I want to try, make it work, to help Leah. But, deep down inside of me, I know. I know that if I do not get out of this marriage ... Bonnie, Leah is capable of anything."

# CHAPTER 30

Despite having someone who supported her, a nice house, a good, steady job, and an education paid for by her husband, Leah could not seem to stay out of trouble. A bit of urine in a cup was her undoing. She had reported for the mandatory meeting with parole, and they asked for a sample to test for drugs.

Leah was notified about the positive results for illegal drugs. "This means," she was told, "You've violated your probation."

When she finally told Ejaz, it was not a good conversation. Time to admit the truth about her background ... well, some of the truth. She had to appear in court.

It was a family gathering but not in a happy sense. Leah, her mother, and Ejaz drove to the federal courthouse in Jackson, Tennessee, a small town just east of Memphis along I45. Upon arrival, they parked and Ejaz told them he was staying in the car. He was not happy and he refused to support this excursion. Leah and her mother went into the courtroom.

It was not good news. Leah was sentenced to serve six months. She was told to report on May 1, 2003. Ejaz was aghast.

Ejaz had always confided in his old friend, Professor Malik. Kafait Malik considered Ejaz a good friend, so he listened to him with concern.

"She is keeping me from my business," Ejaz explained. "And she will not leave me alone, and then I do not know where she is."

"She just goes?" Kafait asked, his eyebrows rising in surprise.

"Where?"

"I do not know, my friend," Ejaz shook his head. "But I have learned something very serious. I do not know what to do, and I am very angry."

"What is it?'

Ejaz sighed. "She is on probation. She was in prison." He let it sink in. "And now she has violated probation. Kafait, what should I do?"

Jordan reports he never saw his father strike Leah, not even in play. He never saw Ejaz push or hit her, never kicked at her or tried to hurt her. He does recall witnessing one argument. "Couples argue," he shrugged. "I just figured, you know, it was normal." Leah raised both her fists and slugged Ejaz in the chest to make a point, and then she stormed off to the bedroom.

Jordan witnessed his father melt a little as his shoulders drooped forward, he dropped his chin, and he sunk down into a chair to stare at the floor with a blank, distant look. There were circles under his eyes, and his swarthy skin had grown pale. Then he asked quietly, "Tariq, do you think I should leave Leah?"

Jordan was taken back. "Why do you want to leave her?"

"Some things are going on. I found out some things about her. What do you think?"

Jordan was eleven years old. He did not know what to say. Looking back, he understood why his father would ask for the little boy's opinion. He wanted Jordan to think about things, to be able to help people and learn to make decisions. Most of all, he understands Ejaz valued his opinions, and was telling him so. Ejaz was usually playful; he loved joking and making Jordan laugh, but he also wanted his son to know how life presented challenges.

Ejaz was torn. He did not want another divorce. He wanted a happy home with his child and his wife. At times, he was determined to make it work and give Leah the benefit of a doubt. He told these things to Bonnie when he telephoned her. But his call to Bonnie after he learned of Leah's previous incarceration truly showed his anger and frustration.

"She is," he told Bonnie in his clipped accent, "a crazy

bitch."

"Ejaz!" Bonnie admonished. "Why would you think that of her? And already!"

"She was in prison, Bonnie," he admitted. "For drugs! I did not know. If I knew this, I would not have married."

"Well," Bonnie tried, "maybe she's okay now."

"No. She steals." Ejaz shared a story of how Leah had taken his prized silver dollar coin collection and spent it. He bemoaned what Leah's children had told him about Leah being still married to the children's father. "And she is on medicine," he added.

"For what?" Bonnie frowned.

"For mental problems," he answered. "When she takes this medicine, she is fine. When she does not, she is crazy and wants to fight. I do not want to fight."

Bonnie did not know what to say. Ejaz was her friend, despite the divorce. They shared a child and they both still respected one another.

Like tectonic plates shifting under his home country, the foundation of Ejaz's world was slowly changing. The movement would not produce good results.

# CHAPTER 31

*"That woman is evil. She is evil!"*
*- Last words spoken by Ejaz Ahmad*
*to a loved one, March 2003*

Each time Ejaz and Bonnie met for visitation exchanges, Bonnie thought Ejaz looked worse than the time before. His thin shoulders bowed inward. He no longer dressed so carefully, and his hair was greasy. There were circles under his eyes. The most telling sign of his sadness, Bonnie now reports, were his eyes.

"You could see turmoil and pain in his eyes," Bonnie explained, years later. "They just weren't ... they weren't dancing and sparkling like they used to be."

"I do not know," he would say. "I want to give Leah chances. But I have tried. I have tried many times."

"Ejaz, you look sick," Bonnie told him bluntly. Even his olive skin had paled.

"I do not know what I am going to do."

"Are you happy?" Bonnie never minced words.

"No," he said without hesitation. "No. She is doing drugs. And she is with someone, I think."

Bonnie had heard that Leah was probably seeing Willie Jackson, who she had heard was Leah's pimp. Bonnie had met Willie only once. She was far from impressed. One of Bonnie's family members owned a string of hotels, some in questionable locations. Some time ago, the family member recognized Leah's photo as the same woman who was walking the corner close to one of the motels, seeking "dates."

"I try to reason," Ejaz was saying, "to talk with her." He sighed heavily, running his hand through his thick hair. "She says she will quit the using, and for a little while, she does good, but then…"

Bonnie looked him in the eyes, eyes that were no longer Ejaz's eyes, which had become the eyes of a haggard old man.

# CHAPTER 32

The family began comparing notes, and sometimes the phones rang constantly while they called one another to talk about Leah and Ejaz.

Johnny Joy still considered Ejaz her brother-in-law despite the divorce, and she loved him like family. She did hear that Leah was on parole, and it surprised her that Ejaz would have anything to do with some criminal. Because of her schedule and the distance she lived away from her family, she did not get to see him often. She saw him in March when he was at Ernestine's house. He was leaving the house, walking to his car. Johnny had just pulled up. "Hey!" She called out to him. "I heard you got married!"

He stopped to shake his head. "Oh, she bad, bad news," he told her as she walked up to greet him. "She lies, Johnny! Oohhh, she lies. I have to get rid of her."

They exchanged a few more words, then Johnny went inside the house and Ejaz drove away. It was the last conversation they had.

"Leah was with him when he stopped the other day," Ernestine Marsh told her daughter. "She looked awful. Pale. She couldn't keep her hands still. You know how she always has her nails done. Well, she was picking the polish off of them." Ernestine shook her head. "I know the signs after all that volunteer work at the women's shelter. She was waiting for that next fix."

"He's a handsome, gorgeous man," Bonnie's sister shook her head. "But he looks so tired now."

In mid March, Ejaz telephoned Bonnie. As usual, the subject was Leah, but this time Ejaz sounded different.

"Bonnie, I cannot take it anymore. I told her, I am going to stay away for a few days."

"From *your* house?"

"Yes. It will give her time to get herself together."

"That's your house, Ejaz!"

"Bonnie, she is a mother," he was adamant. "I cannot make her leave to be on the street."

"Well," Bonnie said, dubious, "let me know what's going on..."

Ejaz could still understand her, knew how she thought. "No, no, I am going to do it. I am through." His voice was so tired, so broken.

They talked a minute or so longer, then said her goodbyes and Bonnie hung up the phone, her eyes filling with tears. *I was right,* she told herself. *That evil bitch has taken him for everything he has.*

Little did she know, a few weeks later, again Bonnie's prediction would come true, worse than she imagined.

Only a few days later Jordan was visiting his dad, and it came time to take him home to Bonnie. Ejaz telephoned Bonnie. "I want you to know we are running late," he explained to her. "I had to stop at the store. I am bringing Tariq home a bit late."

"That's fine," Bonnie told him. "Thanks for calling me." They said their goodbyes.

It was the last time they would speak.

When Jordan came home, he gave Bonnie a big hug. He told her he had a good time. Ejaz had dropped him off without coming in. He still respected the fact Bonnie was married, and Ejaz still felt he should not come into their home.

Finally, Ejaz truly was taking action. Enough of his bank account dwindling, enough of their screaming arguments, enough of the secrets and lies. Towards the end of March he told Leah she had to change her ways or move out.

She moved out. She packed her bags, rounded up her things, and prepared to move on with her life. At least, that's what she told him.

Ejaz drove her to the most expensive hotel in Memphis. He gave her a considerable amount of money and wished her the best. It was the least he could do. She had kids, after all.

You cannot just dump someone's mother out on the street.

Much later, Leah told people they had gone to the hotel so she could complete a job application. Family members and legal representatives questioned this explanation. Leah was working as an aide and planned to continue her education, to attend nursing school. Ejaz was paying for everything she owned. Why would she want to give it all up to go work at a hotel?

Ejaz telephoned Ernestine sometime in late March of 2003. He was frantic, sounding as if he was near tears over the line. It seemed Leah had left, only to return when Ejaz was not at home.

"Ejaz, calm down!" Ernestine told him. "What is going on?"

"It is Leah!" he raged. "That bitch has broken into my home! She has a key – "

"How on earth did she get a key?!"

"She made a copy!" He was frothing mad. "She is stealing! She has taken money out of my account! She has taken some of my things!"

"I tell you what you need to do, Ejaz," Ernestine told him. "Go down to the courthouse and fill out a restraining order against her. Tell them everything that's going on, and fill out the paperwork right then and there."

It took him a moment to compose himself. "What is 'restraining order'?"

Ernestine explained it to him. "Take someone with you that can help you," she advised.

He was breathing hard, but he was listening, she could tell. "But what if ..."

"Ejaz, it's the only legal way you're gonna keep her away from you," his ex-mother-in-law advised. "So if she shows up again, they'll arrest her."

He considered it. They talked a few more minutes. He said he would get a friend and they would go to the courthouse where he would complete the paperwork for a restraining order against Leah.

Before they hung up, Ejaz told Ernestine, "That woman is evil. She is evil!"

Those were the last words a loved one would ever hear Ejaz say.

# CHAPTER 33

*"She is not the person I thought she was."*
*- Ejaz Ahmad to a friend, Mid-April, 2002*

Ejaz had asked his friend Walid Salam to help him sell a car. About March 28, Ejaz drove up into the parking lot of Trade Autos, located on Sumner Street in Memphis, to meet with Walid. Ejaz wanted to sell his current vehicle, a white Lincoln Town Car. A representative from the dealership looked the car over and said, "I'll give you $1,200."

Ejaz refused the offer.

A few days later, on April 2, Ejaz called Walid, who was at an auto auction buying and selling cars. "Can you sell the Lincoln for me at the auction?" he asked.

"I cannot, I have to leave," Walid said, but he gave his friend the number for a dealer.

Johnny Smith, Jr., hung up the telephone again. He did not understand what was going on. He had tried to call Ejaz and instead received a very strange reply.

Johnny had returned from Florida in mid-March and in early April had finally been able to call Ejaz. He wanted to talk to his best friend to catch up on everything. He telephoned Ejaz, expecting to have a long conversation with a lot of laughing. Instead, Leah answered, and she hung up on him. He promptly called back. Leah promptly hung up on him again.

When Leah finally answered the phone, Johnny told her, "Hey, let me talk to Ejaz!"

"He's not here," she said abruptly. "He's gone to Pakistan." *Click.*

Johnny frowned at the telephone. He knew that wasn't true. Since September 11, 2001, Ejaz hasn't been willing to travel to Pakistan. Travel to and from the Middle East, and

Middle Eastern travelers, were closely scrutinized. Ejaz had said he felt safer staying in the U.S.

Leah's snippy attitude was not really a shocker; Johnny knew how she could be.

Johnny later suggested to a friend that someone needed to go to Ejaz's home to find out what was going on. He had no means of transportation – the car Ejaz gave him never ran and he was never able to find the money for repairs – so he was stuck.

Frank Afflitto, a friend of Ejaz, was staying in one of Ejaz's many rental properties, a house located on Wilburn Street in Memphis. As with his home on Sea Isle, Ejaz stored cars at this rental property. He had continued to purchase cars and have them repaired in order to sell them. One car was a white Mitsubishi Mirage. Another was a Ford Taurus.

On April 1, a Pakistani man came to Frank's home; he had purchased the Taurus from Leah and wanted to pick it up. Frank thought it strange that Leah had conducted the transaction and not Ejaz. "How is Ejaz?" Frank asked the man.

"He is in Pakistan," the man told him.

"What?!"

"Yes," the man shrugged. "And I heard his wife has turned herself in to federal authorities."

Tarsha Lilly's home was across the street from the Ahmad home. They all waved politely when they saw one another. About a week into April, Leah approached Tarsha and spoke to her. Leah wanted to sell all of the furniture in the Ahmad's home, and was wondering if her neighbor was interested in purchasing the furniture. Leah told Tarsha that Ejaz was out of town. A short time later, Tarsha saw a panel moving truck at the Ahmad home.

Yared Tedesse was a "Muslim brother" of Ejaz. Like Ejaz and several of his friends, Yared worked as an entrepreneur. He also sold cars. Yared was at an auto auction on April 9, seeking cars he thought would have resell value. He perused various styles of vehicles, sedans, trucks, sports cars, and convertibles. It was possible to do some repairs on some of the cars, and some were not worth the money or the time. It could be difficult to find and keep a good mechanic, so this factored into his decisions as well. This made Yared recall a conversation he had with Ejaz.

Yared knew an African American man who said his name was Carlos, who fancied himself a mechanic but had little knowledge of engines. Nevertheless, Ejaz hired him to work on cars. "Why do you want to have anything to do with Carlos?" Yared had finally demanded of Ejaz. "He is always messing with you. He does not know what he is doing. You should take your cars to a shop where cars are repaired."

Ejaz shrugged. "Carlos' prices are good," Ejaz told him. "And he needs help. He needs the money."

Yared scoffed and rolled his eyes.

On April 10, Yared spoke with Ejaz and met with him in person. They agreed to discuss business further, so spoke on the telephone the following day, during the morning. "We can meet at four o'clock," Ejaz told him, "later today."

It was the last time Yared spoke to his friend.

Yared waited for Ejaz. Soon, 3:30 p.m. came and went, and then the clock ticked to four o'clock. No Ejaz. Yared checked his wristwatch several times. Ejaz was already an hour late. This was so unlike Ejaz, and it was unheard of for him to not call or show up to meet. Yared called the house, and Leah answered. Yared asked if she had any idea about Ejaz missing their meeting.

"I don't know," came the curt reply. "But he's gone to Pakistan now, so I can't ask him."

It was around April 14, Jordan later explained to investigators, when Ejaz and Leah stopped by the home he shared with his mother and grandmother. During their chatter, Ejaz had asked Jordan, "Do you want to stay this weekend with me?" Jordan was unsure; he was supposed to go see a hospitalized relative. Sometime before midnight,

Jordan arrived home from the visit when Ejaz called him. As they spoke, Ejaz asked, "Tariq, did you decide if you want to stay this weekend with me?"

"I can't," Jordan told Ejaz. "I'm helping grandma with some things."

Ejaz talked to his son for a little longer. He was happy Tariq was a responsible boy who wanted to help his family. It was the right thing to do. Ejaz always believed a person should do the right thing.

A friend named Hassam would later recall a conversation he had with Ejaz in early to mid April. Hassam worshipped at the same mosque. Ejaz was obviously distraught, not his usual smiling self.

"I am not happy with my wife," Ejaz confided to Hassam bitterly.

"What is wrong?"

"We had a ceremony to be married, I am not sure if it was legal. I think she is still married to someone else. And …" He took a deep breath. "She is not at all the person I thought she was. Hassam, I need to get away. Away from her."

# CHAPTER 34

A pawn shop is a mix-match of various and sundry items which people either have to get rid of, just don't want anymore, or they need cash more than they need the item. A pawn shop promises fast cash for almost anything. Some pawn shop employees do a bit more than what they have to.

The pawn shop Cash America enters information into their computer system such as a driver's license number and all information on the license. They also have the person give a fingerprint for identification. Leah Ward walked into a Cash America pawnshop on April 17 around 1:00 p.m. She presented a ring she wanted to pawn for fast cash. It was stunning; a man's ring of "22 karat yellow gold," the "diamond total weight: 5.6 (carats)."[6] The employee looked it over and told Leah she would get $40. She agreed. Leah's driver license showed an address in Cordova, Tennessee, one of her many former addresses. The employee who assisted Leah entered this address into Cash America's identification system; Leah said nothing about the Cordova address being old, that she no longer lived there and had not lived in Cordova for years. She signed a legal document stating the ring was her own, carefully pressed her inked thumbprint onto the document, and stuck the pawn ticket and two twenty-dollar bills in her purse.

Later, investigators learned the ring was the legal property of Ejaz Ahmad. He had it custom made, and had already promised it to his son for when Jordan got older.

The Cordova address Leah gave was also shared with a man named Oke. Both Leah's car and Oke's car were registered to this address. Oke was a member of a royal family in his native country, but in the United States Oke had a criminal record.

Ejaz did not have a cellphone, so any communication

6   Cash America #4 Ticket # P15952-1-1, 04/17/2003

with him was usually through the phone in his house.

Leah did have a cellphone, and on April 23, Leah phoned Jordan from her cellphone. "I'm on my way to Jackson," she told him, "to get Christopher and Sallie."

"Can I speak to my father?"

"Oh, I'm sorry," she replied. "He's out of town."

That following day Leah again phoned Jordan from her cell phone. They chatted, and Leah told Jordan, "Your dad is in Little Rock, picking up a car."

"I'll call him later, then," Jordan sighed.

"Oh, well, he'll be gone for a few days," Leah told him.

And again, on April 25, Leah called both Jordan and Bonnie from her cell phone.

Jordan put one of the calls on speakerphone. Ernestine Marsh was passing by when she caught a bit of their conversation.

"Yeah, your daddy's in Pakistan," Leah's cheerful voice carried through the speaker. "I would sure love to go there one day. Maybe I'll get to go." She hesitated, and then sighed. "I don't know ... I think I'm going to Florida, shave my head ... just get lost."

Jordan had no response for that comment.

Ernestine heard Leah say something about "half brothers and sisters." She didn't linger, in order to not eavesdrop, feeling it would be intrusive.

Jordan finally handed the phone to his mother. While Bonnie was talking to Leah, Jordan said something to his grandmother about the "half brothers and sisters" discussion.

"I wonder if she's pregnant," Ernestine mused.

"I think she was talking about Christopher and Sallie," he told her.

"Oh no, honey," Ernestine explained, "They're called a 'step' brother and sister."

"Oh."

Meanwhile, Bonnie was on the phone with Leah. "Where is Ejaz?" Bonnie asked her. "Jordan wants to talk with him.

They haven't talked in a while."

"Oh, he's in West Memphis, picking up a car," came the breezy reply. "He'll be back in a few days."

"Okay," Bonnie told her. "Well, please have him call us when he gets back, okay?"

"He'll be gone for two weeks," Leah amended.

On April 26, Leah signed a rental agreement at 9:00 a.m. for a 15' parcel van from Budget, paying $240.00 in cash. She agreed the truck would be returned on April 28th by 8:00 a.m. Leah also burned up hours on her cell phone talking to both Jordan and Bonnie. She called a number of times. She would speak to Jordan at length, and then she spoke to Bonnie. She even hung up, and called back some time later. "Me and Ejaz had a fight the day before he left," she finally told Bonnie, her voice sounding sad.

"Where is he now?" Bonnie wondered aloud.

"Pakistan."

"What!" Bonnie almost fell over. "Why would he not tell us? Leah, Ejaz would tell us if he went home. And why did you lie and say he was in Arkansas?"

"He wants a divorce," Leah's voice travelled over the airwaves. "And he wants me gone when he gets back from Pakistan. I've lost a lotta weight, Bonnie. I'm so worried – about him – that I've lost weight. He's been gone two weeks now, and he won't come back 'til another two weeks."

Bonnie did not know what to say.

"Bonnie," Leah's voice was so final. "I have to tell you. I – I'm so insecure. Really. And I know I'm never gonna measure up to the kind of woman you are … and not the kind of woman Ejaz is used to. You'll always know him," she sniffed. "You'll *always* know him better than I ever will."

Bonnie rolled her eyes, while noticing Leah's flat and emotionless tone. "Leah, are you crazy or what? That's bullshit."

Then came a curt response. "Yeah. When I see him I'll tell him that." *Click.*

Jordan approached her a bit later. "Mom," he said carefully, "Leah didn't want to tell you ... she's pregnant."

Dan Simone and his family were renting a house from Ejaz Ahmad, so he was not surprised when Ejaz's wife showed up at his front door, but he was shocked at what she told him.

"You have to get out," Leah told the tenant. "You need to move."

Dan Simone did eventually move out, but before he had the chance to start packing, someone broke into his home. The only items stolen were baby clothes.

Later, it would be discovered that Leah had committed the burglary. By then it did not matter, because she was facing far more serious charges.

Leah had stopped by the Wilburn Street house that Frank Afflitto was renting. She was driving Ejaz's white Lincoln. Frank greeted her and politely acknowledged the two women with her. He was shocked that Ejaz's wife would know these people, for they were unsavory types, suspicious appearing woman who dressed trashy. Frank acknowledged to himself that it was certainly not his business what type of people Leah Ahmad ran with.

It was not the first time Frank had been shocked by someone he saw accompanying Leah. There was a black man named "Carlos" who worked at a friend's auto shop and also worked for Ejaz. Frank had heard a rumor that Carlos and Leah had been arrested together in February. He had heard that they both stayed a week behind bars. Carlos was known to smoke a lot of crack, among other shady dealings.

Leah would visit the Wilburn house again, once again surprising Frank Afflitto. Leah was with a different woman this time, and again she was driving Ejaz's white Lincoln. Frank welcomed them but was shocked by what he saw. Gone was the hijab, the conservative dress. Leah was clad in a halter-top and tight pants that showed every curve. She wore makeup. She was smoking cigarettes, which Frank had never seen her do when she was with Ejaz. The woman she was with did not look like a respected member of any society; she was far too skinny – sickly skinny -- and did not seem to care about her looks. Leah told Frank she was there to pick up the Mitsubishi Mirage, and Frank saw no reason to question her. He watched Leah drive off in the Mitsubishi, and the skinny woman follow her in the Lincoln.

In late April, Frank spoke briefly with a man named Nabil; they worshipped at the same mosque as Ejaz. They began asking one another about mutual friends.

"You know, I was looking for Ejaz," Nabil mentioned. "I went by his home."

"Did you see him?" Frank asked.

"No. His wife said he was in Pakistan."

It didn't seem unusual, for he knew Ejaz went to Pakistan to see family, spend time at home, and sometimes would purchase items to sell in the States. Frank nodded, and the conversation turned.

Sometime after April 29, Frank came home to find his house was stripped of all furnishings. There was also a note from Leah; the note read that the new renters would be moving into the house in two days. Frank moved into a room at the mosque temporarily so he would have a place to live while searching for another rental house.

When Ashad opened his front door, he could not believe who stood on his doorstep.

She was dressed in tight, short shorts, her breasts threatened to tumble out of her sheer blouse. Ashad thought she looked like a prostitute, but it was Ejaz's wife.

Ejaz and Ashad had met while in school, and remained good friends. Ashad shared the same devout Muslim beliefs as Ejaz. He was astonished that this woman was Ejaz's wife, in her provocative, cheap clothing.

"Listen," Leah was telling him, in a friendly tone, "You don't have to pay rent to Ejaz anymore. Just pay it directly to me."

"Okay, yes, I can do that."

They exchanged a few pleasantries and she left, striding back to her car.

*That was strange*, Ashad thought.

Johnny Joy telephoned her mother, finally able to find some time where she could just sit down and have a long conversation, and was shocked by the news she received.

"Ejaz is missing," Ernestine told her worriedly.

"What?"

"He's missing. We can't find him anywhere!"

Johnny was not sure she heard correctly. "What do you mean he's 'missing'? Ejaz can't be missing!"

"We can't get a hold of him," The worry in Ernestine's voice was unmistakable. "Bonnie, me, Jordan – we've all tried."

Jordan tried calling his father again. Again, Leah answered. Jordan put her on speakerphone and Ernestine listened in.

"Well, like I told you, your daddy's in West Memphis," she was saying.

"But I called and something was wrong with the house phone," Jordan told Leah.

"Ohhh. Well, we're not getting along. We had a fight and he jerked the phone out of the wall."

Jordan and Ernestine merely stared at one another.

"I'll tell him to call you." *Click.*

Deborah and Jerry Moore had resided on Sea Isle for over ten years. They had noticed Ejaz moving in, and, on occasion, Deborah saw him in the neighborhood. They never spoke, but if their eyes met they smiled and nodded at each other. When she came home from work, Deborah often saw Leah. It was never really anything to note, just casual observation of a neighbor.

The people living on Sea Isle street were familiar with Ejaz's home; there were always cars for sale parked in the driveway and in the street. It seemed as soon as one car was taken away, another car took its place. Some of the cars seemed to need a lot of work. Jerry Moore had noted an African American man working on one of the cars in early April, but it was only enough to note and nothing to warrant further thought. .

Deborah did note when the cars had all been removed in late April and a large moving van was parked on the Ahmad front lawn from about April 25th to around the 29th. The driver's side of the truck was closest to the house. She did not see anyone, but guessed, after five year's residency, that her neighbor was now moving out, but she did not put much thought into it. Sometime during these five days, she did see the woman of the house spraying something with the garden hose. Deborah was too far away to see anything else. Deborah mentioned it to Jerry. "I guess we'll have new neighbors soon. I never saw the ones living there now," he told her. "Well, the wife. She's always dressed up. And I've seen their kids." Jerry had only noted the moving van's arrival on the 27th or 28th, he later told investigators. He also reported that he saw the wife spraying off the driver's side of the moving truck at around 8:00 a.m. on the 29th.

Meanwhile, Leah called the federal probation offices. She told them she needed to surrender for violation of probation. "I don't have any money," she told them. "So I have no way to even get there. I don't even have a car!"

"Is there someone who can bring you?"

"No."

Leah was told that she needed to contact the U.S. Marshall's office, and she agreed that was a good idea, but knew first that she had a lot of things to take care of before she went to jail.

# CHAPTER 35

Monday, April 28, was a busy day for Leah Ward.

She went to Storage USA, the same location where she rented the moving truck, at 10:00 a.m. There, she signed the rental agreement for a 10' by 15' storage unit. She paid for a six-month lease at $57.50 per month and paid $400.00 in cash: She wrote down her alternative contact as "Jane Doe, phone number 555-1212." Leah noted that she would be storing "3 bedroom house full 3 beds furniture, antiques, house items, clothes." She listed the total value of the items at $4,999.00. While she was unloading items from the truck to the storage unit, employees at Storage USA casually noted a man and a woman assisting her.

On that same Monday, at about 7:30 a.m., neighbor Catherine Long departed her home in the 1700 block of Sea Isle as she was going to work. She noted a yellow Ryder moving truck parked on the lawn at the Ahmad residence. When she came home from work that day, Catherine noted the truck was still parked at Ejaz's home.

The next day, the 29th of April, a Tuesday, Catherine left for work and noted the truck still remained at Ejaz's home, parked across the lawn blocking a front window and the front door of the house. When Catherine came home for lunch, she glanced over at Ejaz's house. She noted a white female wearing blue jeans, a white shirt, and white tennis shoes. The woman's blonde hair was in a ponytail. She was under the hood of a small, light colored compact car, apparently showing it to several people who were standing nearby, and who also milled around, looking at the other cars parked in the yard.

As Catherine thought about it, she realized she had not seen Ejaz in about a month. Jordan was a good friend of Catherine's son Denny, and they played together whenever Jordan was at his dad's house.

She wondered if the blonde woman was Ejaz's wife; she matched the description Denny had once given Catherine.

Catherine wondered if the activity at the Ahmad house meant that the family was moving. Denny had gone to Ejaz's home a few days ago, returning dejected. He told his mom that Ejaz's wife had answered the door and told him Ejaz had gone back to Pakistan, so Jordan wouldn't be over for some time.

Catherine later recalled a horrible smell coming from Ejaz's back yard, near her yard. Her boyfriend Bryan had checked her own yard, thinking maybe the cat had killed something. The smell was really bad on Wednesday, and she asked Bryan if he had forgotten to put the trash out.

On Monday, April 28, Walid Salam's employees were, as usual, tending to the Vance Avenue car lot and repair center when Leah Ward came bursting through the door. She was visibly shaking, sweaty, and barely able to control herself. The employees placed a phone call to Walid, explaining that Ejaz's wife was at the shop, wanting to sell a car.

Walid arrived at the car lot. "Where is she?" he asked. Someone pointed out the blonde woman.

"He's gone to Pakistan and left me no money!" She shouted. "He won't be back for a week … or two weeks."

Walid had her sit down. "What happened?" he gently asked her.

"He's gone to Pakistan and left me stranded!" She could barely sit still. "I need money."

They struck a deal when Walid agreed to give her $300 for the white Mitsubishi Mirage she was driving. That seemed to calm her down, but not much. He told her he could get the money to her the next day.

"I have a Lincoln I need fixed," she told him, mopping the sweat from her brow. "Can you get someone to come over?"

He agreed to help out, because Ejaz was his friend, and he wanted to help him any way he could.

"Can you take me to a tire shop?" Leah asked him, since she no longer had transportation, having just sold her ride. "It's on Lamar, near McLean."

Walid agreed and drove her to the tire shop, but a sign on the door and the locked bars indicated the shop was closed.

"Well," she sighed, "can you take me home?"

Walid obliged, driving her home.

"Listen, I have those junked cars we need to sell," she told Walid as they pulled up to the house. "I want to get rid of them, too."

Walid agreed to purchase them and told her he would return the next day to complete the sales, with money in hand.

As agreed, the next day, Walid arrived at Ejaz's home, where Leah met him outside.

Walid looked over the three vehicles parked on his friend's property. They were salvage vehicles, not worth much. None of them even ran, and all would have to be towed. "I'll move them to my lot," he told her. "I will pay you $300 for the three junked cars, in addition to the $300 for the Mitsubishi that we talked about yesterday."

Leah agreed and a bill of sale was completed. Walid tucked the bill of sale into his shirt pocket. "When Ejaz comes back, he can have his junk back," he muttered to himself. "I am just trying to help out here."

Deborah Moore was retrieving the newspaper from the front lawn of her home on Sea Isle when she saw the woman at the Ahmad home. Deborah had a brief thought that it was unusual to see her that time of day; she only saw the blonde in the evening when Deborah was pulling onto the street, coming home from work. This time, the woman was carrying a box, walking quickly, to a four door black car that looked like a Cadillac. The trunk was raised and the doors were open on the car. Deborah thought nothing more of what she saw … until later. For now, it was 6:00 a.m. and time for coffee.

On April 30, Leah called Walid. She reminded him about the broken down Lincoln, and wondered when he would be able to come over with his mechanic?

Shortly after the call, Walid arrived with his mechanic, a man named Bobby. The mechanic did some repair work on the Lincoln Town Car. Bobby was able to get the car running.

"While you're here," Leah asked both men, "can you help me move some boxes?"

Walid and Bobby followed her into the home and were immediately struck by a powerfully pungent odor. Walid pinched his nose. "Ugh!"

Bobby was grimacing. "What is that?"

"It's meat in the refrigerator that went bad," Leah told him. "I have to throw it out. The refrigerator went out."

The men quickly helped lift the boxes and put them in the trunk of the Lincoln, as she had requested. They departed swiftly in order to escape the horrible smell.

Bonnie Garrett consulted with her brother. Something was not right, and she still had not heard from Ejaz. Not a single call, note, not any form of communication. Jordan missed his father, spending time together and talking on the telephone. He missed his pet hen, feeding and caring for her. He was worried the chicken was not being cared for.

So on April 30, Bonnie and her brother drove to Ejaz's house, where they parked on the street, and slowly walked up the sidewalk, looking about. The lawn needed mowing and the shrubs were unkempt, which was odd. Ejaz always tended to his home. Bonnie assumed it was because he had been away as Leah had told them. Bonnie knocked on the door. Even if it was Leah who answered, Bonnie had reasoned that at least she could confront her in person. She checked her watch, it was exactly 1:15 p.m. "All the blinds are closed," she noted aloud, knocking again. "That's weird." She pressed her nose to the only window that afforded a view of the inside of the house. "The furniture's gone!" she exclaimed.

There was a car sitting at an angle under the carport. Bonnie looked it over as she pounded on Ejaz's side door. The car was so filthy she could barely tell its color.

Bonnie walked toward the back of the house and was about to cross into the back yard when she glanced at the shed. Then a strange thing happened that, today, she can only try to explain.

"My knees just seemed to lock up. I could not go in that backyard. My feet would not even move." A creepy chill pulled her shoulders back, and then traveled down her spine, causing her to violently shiver. When she was finally able to move, she turned away to get out of there, rushing back to the car.

When she returned to where her car was parked along the sidewalk, she told her brother, "Nobody's here. Even the furniture is gone! Let's try the mosque." She did not want to tell him about her strange feeling of not being able to go into the back yard, for fear of being laughed at.

"Tell me how to get to the mosque," he replied, mentally trying to process the information she'd relayed about the missing furniture.

She directed him to the corner of Mynders Street and Highland.

The Imam, the Muslim equivalent of a priest or preacher in other faiths, warmly greeted Bonnie. Two men joined him as they spoke.

"We have not seen Ejaz for about three or four weeks," they told her. She received the same answer as she asked around the mosque. They smiled, and tried to help, but none of his friends knew where he could be.

Dispirited and frightened for Ejaz, she drove home with her brother.

Sometime after her search at the mosque, Bonnie tried to file a missing persons report, but was told by law enforcement that it could not be filed because Ejaz didn't meet the necessary criteria to have a missing person's report filed. He was an adult, and therefore considered of an age where he could come and go as he pleased. There was no evidence that he was a possible harm to himself, he wasn't suffering a known medical or psychological crisis, and there was no known sign of foul play.

The officer asked her how did she know that he was not overseas?

"I just have a feeling," she told the officer.

He looked at her askance. This was Memphis, Tennessee, and if officers investigated every "feeling," they would never leave work.

While Bonnie was knocking on the door of her ex-husband's home, Leah was surrendering herself to the U.S. Marshall's offices. On April 30, she walked into the doors of a federal holding facility and was processed in. The officer noted on her paperwork that she was to be transferred to a federal women's prison on May 5.

Not so bad, Leah told herself as she settled into a holding cell to wait. She had been in worst predicaments.

# CHAPTER 36

Johnny Smith, Jr., was able to learn a few things about the days in April. From what he heard, it seemed Ejaz had friends in town who were staying at a high priced Memphis hotel. Leah had told others she was dropping off an application for employment. Officials believe Ejaz and Leah had agreed she was to leave him and he was dropping Leah off to get her out of his life, and it was not in his nature to just dump her on the street. Whatever the truth, it is known that Ejaz drove Leah to the hotel.

It is believed that Leah either hid Ejaz's bag of important papers, or she threatened to do so, so they began arguing. Leah took the car and drove off, leaving Ejaz fuming in the hotel parking lot.

When Ejaz finally arrived at the house, she had locked all the doors and he did not have his keys so he could not let himself in. He began to bang on the doors and windows, shouting at her to let him in. This was an altered version of the story Leah would later repeat in a legal statement.

Law enforcement was never able to ascertain if Leah Ward had ever actually applied for employment at the hotel.

Sometime during her search, Bonnie went to a trusted friend who read Tarot cards in order to try to gain some insight. The friend reluctantly told her, "I have a vision of him rolled up in a rug." The two women looked at one another and burst into tears.

Finally, Ernestine Marsh had about enough of all the mystery. She decided to go to Ejaz's house and find out just exactly what was going on. At the last minute, Jordan asked if he could go, and she agreed, as they set out for the brick home on Sea Isle Street. It was May 1, 2003.

*Ejaz Ahmad was an educated, self-made man who came to
America from Pakistan. He had many talents: art, electronics,
salesmanship, cooking; his biggest joy came from being
with his family and friends. (Courtesy Jordan Ahmad)*

*Bonnie and Ejaz met and it was love at first sight. "Once you have something like that," Bonnie explains, "no one can replace it." (Courtesy Jordan Ahmad)*

*Ernestine Marsh was Ejaz's mother-in-law and, in many ways, his surrogate mother. She keeps a photograph of Ejaz with baby Jordan, seen here over her left shoulder, in a prominent place in her home. (Courtesy Ernestine Marsh)*

*Ejaz and his son, Jordan. "My dad taught me everything,"
Jordan remembers. (Courtesy Jordan Ahmad)*

*Ejaz was a constant in Jordan's life. On one of their trips to
Pakistan, they went for a camel ride. (Courtesy Jordan Ahmad)*

*Ejaz Ahmad and Leah Ward. "She's going to take everything he's got," predicted a loved one. (Courtesy Jordan Ahmad)*

*Ejaz Ahmad after a few months of living with Leah. He had lost his self-assurance and the sparkle in his eyes. (Courtesy Jordan Ahmad)*

*The Ahmad home bathroom where Leah hid the body*
*for weeks before placing it in the shed. (Courtesy of*
*Shelby County District Attorney General's Office)*

*Leah hid the remains in this shed, located in Ejaz's back yard. Neighbors complained of the smell. (Courtesy of Shelby County District Attorney General's Office)*

*Searching for clues as to his whereabouts, Ejaz Ahmad's remains were found by his family. (Photo augmented for privacy) (Courtesy of Shelby County District Attorney General's Office)*

*Ejaz's family agreed, "Leah was pretty, but there was something about her." Someone close to Ejaz summed it up: "She was a vicious, conniving snake." (Courtesy Jordan Ahmad)*

*Leah Ward's identification tag when she worked as a PCA for a Memphis hospital. (Courtesy of Shelby County District Attorney General's Office)*

*Mug shot of Leah Joy Ward during her earlier criminal career. (Courtesy of Shelby County District Attorney General's Office)*

*September 2003 mug shot of Leah Joy Ward after her arrest for the murder of Ejaz Ahmad. (Courtesy of Memphis Police Department)*

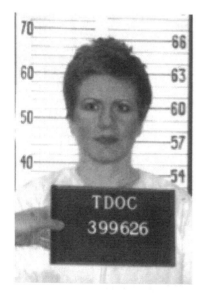

*Leah Joy Ward in her 2012 prison mug shot at age 38. She is currently incarcerated at the Tennessee Prison for Women. She will be released in 2059, when she is 83 years old. (Courtesy of the Tennessee Department of Corrections)*

*As a new Assistant District Attorney, Pamela Fleming assisted in the successful conviction of Leah Joy Ward. The Ward case remains one of her most memorable. (Author's collection)*

# CHAPTER 37

*"I wrapped the head in a little sheet and put it in a black plastic bag like a garbage bag ... I threw it in a big dumpster ... I don't know where it was at."*
*- Leah Joy Ward's confession to Sergeant Sims and Detective Webb, Memphis Police Department, May 5, 2003*

On May 3, 2003, two days after Ejaz's dead body was discovered, Bonnie, accompanied by her mother and her son, and walked into the Memphis Police Department's Homicide Office at 201 Poplar Avenue, in order to give their statements.

Law enforcement officials found Ernestine Marsh to be a bright, charismatic, and gregarious woman. She told investigators about her background in law enforcement, she has penned award-winning songs, and she was quite involved with the Elvis Birthday Celebration every year, one of the biggest bashes in Memphis. At age seventy-two, with her stylish hats and outfits, she had more energy and personality than many people. But the loss of Ejaz, her "son," had caused worry lines around her once-bright eyes and big smile.

"Even though I'm his ex mother-in-law, we still talked frequently, we always got along fine," she said of Ejaz. She remembered going to the house just two days prior, how Jordan had ran to her car to ask where she was going and if he could tag along. "Well, go tell your mother," Ernestine had told the boy.

She vividly recalled most details. She remembered walking up to the house and knocking on the door, speaking with the neighbors, and seeing the chicken.

The next part of her story was difficult to tell. Years later, it still brings tears to her eyes.

After lifting the egg crate mattress, Ernestine told them she saw a man's bottom. "I knew it was part of a human, so I lowered (the mattress) and didn't want Jordan to see it. I thought in my mind, 'it's Jordan's dad.'" She dabbed her eyes with a tissue. "We went back to the house across the street and told them to call 9-1-1." By the time the police arrived, Ernestine remembered she was sitting on the porch, with the kindly neighbor holding a cold compress to Ernestine's forehead to keep her from fainting.    "Jordan was kinda in shock," her voice warbled, as she described Jordan's reaction to what was happening around him.

One thing she was sure of was that Ejaz was gone. He was gone forever.

She recalled Ejaz and Leah's visit to her home on April 14. Leah "looked unkempt," she recalled. It was the last time she had seen or spoken to Leah.

The investigators had shown her a photograph of the ring Leah had pawned at Cash America. She thought it looked similar to one Ejaz wore, but she could not be sure.

Bonnie had to sit in on Jordan's interview, as he was a minor. The little boy with grief-rimmed eyes was polite, articulate, and sat up straight in his chair. It was obvious he was wise beyond his years. He told Sergeants Sims and Oliver he attended middle school and was in sixth grade. He acknowledged that he was aware there was an investigation into Ejaz's death.

"I don't know who (killed him)," Jordan said. Despite admitting Leah was "nice" to him, he had asserted, "I think it's Leah Ward, because she moved out all of her stuff." He told investigators his last contact with his father was "about three weeks ago." He told the investigators about accompanying his grandmother, trying to catch the hen, and the discovery of his beloved father's body on May 1; he guessed at about 5:30 p.m.

The shed was never locked, Jordan explained pragmatically, because the hen's nest was in the shed, and she laid her eggs in there. He told how she would bob her head, clucking, at the motorcycle, parts from various cars, oil cans, and miscellaneous junk as she headed for the nest.

He told them about Leah's mixed messages when they spoke on the telephone, and about the guns at the house. "He owns swords and two guns ... one BB gun and one shotgun or rifle." Jordan told them he never actually saw the guns; they just came up in conversations. He did admit that he knew where Ejaz kept money hidden in the home.

The investigators showed him a photo of the ring that Leah had pawned. It looked familiar, and may have been on a table in Ejaz's bedroom, but Jordan was not sure.

His father and Leah "argued all the time," Jordan admitted. "She was manic-depressive. When she wouldn't take her medication, she started fights with my dad." He responded that he knew his father had many friends, but he did not know their names.

What about his last conversation with Ejaz?

"He wanted me to stay the weekend with him."

Bonnie had a folder full of papers that she held in a tight clutch when she met with Sergeant Howell. Howell carefully looked at the folder. Inside were bank account numbers, notations, and a list of addresses and phone numbers for Ejaz's relatives in Pakistan. Howell sat down to speak with Bonnie. Bonnie told the investigator about Ejaz's telephone call in November 2002. "Ejaz told me that Leah was a crazy bitch," she said flatly. She explained Leah's strange calls through the month of April. Bonnie had a good memory, and she could recall dates and times with ease. She painfully went through the evening of May 1st. She told them of a ring Ejaz had custom made especially for their son. On the way to the police station, they had discussed that ring, and Jordan told her he had never received the ring. Jordan also told her that, according to Ejaz, there was a pellet gun and a rifle in the house. "Ejaz also had a lot of Pakistani knives and swords," Bonnie said.

After their talk, Sergeant Howell ensured the office had copies of the file's contents for their case folder. A copy of Ejaz's will was also among the documents.

On that same Saturday, neighbor Catherine Long told Sergeant Sims about seeing a yellow moving truck at her neighbor's home on April 28. The interview only lasted a bit over fifteen minutes, but it provided corroboration for other witness statements, which all combined to help build the case and seal the fate of Leah Joy Ward.

# CHAPTER 38

Lieutenant Norris and his team interviewed Leah's coworkers. Nothing of investigative value came from those interviews.

Norris discovered Leah had violated her parole with a drug charge, and she had turned herself in as ordered. He placed a call to the U.S. Marshall's offices, requesting she not be transported from the federal holding facility, placing a hold on the move. Instead, he explained, Leah Joy Ward needed to be transported from the federal holding facility to the Shelby County Justice Center in downtown Memphis.

Leah had convinced herself she was safe. She thought she had secured her alibi, as she was in a federal holding facility in Mason, Tennessee, preparing to be transferred to a minimum-security faculty to do her time for the parole violation. She smugly believed that in just a few months, she would be out of jail and back in the free world. She was still confident when the U.S. Marshalls showed up on May 5, 2003 to transport her to the Memphis Police Department for questioning about a murder.

The Marshalls transported Leah to the Shelby County Justice Center in downtown Memphis. She was about to be interviewed about the death of Ejaz Ahmad.

Upon arrival, they entered the ground floor of the tall, cool building. An officer pushed the button to open the doors of the elevator and they entered. The officer pushed the button for the eleventh floor, the elevator doors closed quietly, and the elevator began its slow ascent, while Leah Ward's world was about to descend.

Leah settled in to speak with Memphis Police Sergeant Sims and Detective Webb. Leah was read her rights and stated she understood each of her rights per the Miranda warning. Then she confessed to murder.

On the day before she killed him, Leah told them, she and

Ejaz went to the hotel so she could pick up an employment application. He was angry, so he sat in the car while she obtained an application. She told Sims and Webb how Ejaz was gone when she came back outside. She returned to the house they shared. She did not explain how she got to the house.

She had taken Ejaz's black bag of personal papers and put them in the car she was currently driving, a white 1995 Mitsubishi Mirage two door. She knew this would make Ejaz blow up, and "he would have to talk to me." After putting them in her car, she went to work at Baptist East Memorial Hospital. After her shift ended, she went to the home of a friend, arriving a little after 11:00 at night. She left her friend's home and returned to her own home, arriving there around 12:00 am to 1:00 am.

She had hoped Ejaz would get angry over his missing bag and he did. They fought loudly, screaming and shouting. He sat on the couch demanding to know where his bag was hidden.

"I don't know," Leah replied tartly.

Ejaz threatened her, she told the investigators. "He said, 'The next time you take those papers or that bag, I will kill you.'"

She went into their bedroom and locked the door.

Leah had a gun, she confessed, and she retrieved it from the top shelf of her daughter's closet. She did not know what kind of gun it was, only that it was small, black, and had a cocking mechanism. She knew it was loaded. She returned to the bedroom she shared with Ejaz and placed the gun under the bed should she need to protect herself.

She told the officers she then went to sleep, until Ejaz woke her at about 6:00 or 7:00 in the morning. Because the bedroom door was locked, he pounded on the door to ask if she was going to school. Leah told him, also through the locked door, that no, she was not going.

"Go get my papers!" he shouted at her. "Go get my bag!"

Ejaz then pounded on the bedroom door with his fists, she told the investigators. Then he started throwing himself against the door, shouting at her. "He busted the door," she told them. "He ...started beating on me, and he asked where the gun was and I said I didn't know. Somehow he left the room and tried to come in through the window." She was not sure if he busted down their door the first time or the second time.

Somewhere in her story, Leah stepped out of the bedroom and went into the bathroom; she locked the door and hid in the bathroom closet.

Enraged, Ejaz took the outside water hose and began spraying the inside of the bathroom through the bathroom window. Then he tried to get into the bathroom via the window.

Exiting the bathroom, she could turn to run down the hall to the front door, or she could turn and run into the bedroom. "I ran into the bedroom and grabbed the gun from underneath the bed, because I noticed that it's getting worse. I kept the gun in my hand, and ... then he comes through the bedroom door and grabs me by the throat and puts me in the corner in the bedroom."

At this point, she was pointing the gun at her husband.

She whispered to the detectives, that as he was choking her, she pulled the trigger.

*Click.*

Ejaz paused, then continued to hit her. She pulled the trigger again, and when the gun went off that time it shocked both of them. Ejaz stepped back, his face a mask of confusion and disbelief, and then "he fell on the bed," mumbling in "Arabic" she told the officers. There was a hole in his chest where the bullet had entered. He then fell to the floor, crying.

"I ran into the living room (and) started praying that God would save him."

She returned to the bedroom, but her prayers were not answered. Ejaz lay dead. "It was at least two-thirty in the evening, because I looked at the time."

She also said she shot him twice. One bullet entered his heart; the other hit him in the stomach. She did not notice it at first. But after a few minutes she noticed that she had "really shot him."

Then "I walked around the neighborhood." That's when she might have thrown the gun away, but she claimed that she just could not remember.

When she returned to the house, it was deathly quiet. She claimed she stayed next to Ejaz's body "for days."

She tried to drag him into the tub, but he was heavy. She managed to get a leg into the tub while his body lay on the bathroom floor. "I covered him with a white sheet," she explained. She removed his trousers and underwear because they had fecal matter and urine on them. "I washed him with a cloth but I couldn't get him in the bathtub."

She would later say she was trying to give him a proper Muslim burial, starting with the washing of the body.

Some days later, the smell of decaying flesh permeated the house. Leah did not recall exactly when, but she went into the bathroom. "It had been weeks," she told them. "The smell was strong and I opened the bathroom door and saw worms coming out of him." She tried to clean up the worms, and then closed the bathroom door. She removed the sheet she had used to cover Ejaz and put it in the garbage.

Eventually, Leah returned to the bathroom, she told Sergeant Sims and Detective Webb. Again, she tried to clean up the blood and worms. She grabbed a hold of him and yanked and pulled, but could not budge his body. She tried to clean up the blood and worms. His body was not moving. Leah said she panicked, and retrieved one of Ejaz's swords from the living room. ("I don't know what size or what color it was," she reported.)

She used it to cut off his head.

She also admitted to removing the penis and testicles. She wrapped the head in a sheet and then dumped it into a trash bag, placed it in her 1995 Mirage, and drove off around "for at least thirty minutes" and then threw Ejaz's head into a dumpster. "I don't know where it was at," she claimed.

Leah admitted to doing the same with the sexual organs, but also just could not seem to recall where she tossed them. Possibly in another dumpster. She just could not remember.

She did not mention any other wounds such as the marks on the femur head where she attempted to cut off his leg. She did not mention any other wounds.

She found a wire cable and a red rope. Using a cable she found, she tied it around one of his legs, and tied a red rope around one of his arms. Grunting with the effort, she finally managed to pull Ejaz out of the bathroom.

Then, using the cable and rope, she drug Ejaz's body out of the front door near midnight. She became "scared" so she dragged the body around the side of the house, through the gate. She dumped him into the shed, where she covered him with an egg crate mattress. "I covered it with some kind of foam thing," she told Sergeant Sims and Detective Webb, "because it was naked."

Leah closed the shed by placing boards over the open doorway. She figured the body was in the shed for two or three days by the time she self-surrendered on April 30th. She said she then cleaned the house and the bathroom window. "Proof will show in the house that there was a struggle."

She explained how she had sold a few cars for $50.00 and pawned a gold ring with a design on it, receiving twenty-five or thirty dollars. "I wasn't trying to gain anything," she sighed. She stored items in an East Memphis U-Storage, prepaying for four months, the time she thought it would take her to serve her jail sentence. Investigators soon found out she wasn't even honest about these details.

Leah told them that she attempted to call 9-1-1 at least once, but she was scared and hung up, because she had killed Ejaz with a gun, which was also a probation violation for her to have one in the house. "I had never harmed anyone before," she said.

She stated that eventually she gave the 1995 Mirage to a junkyard in South Memphis, near downtown.[7]

She killed him in self-defense, Leah told them, because she feared for her life that day. She asserted that she was a battered woman, suffering a lifetime of abuse by her father, her husband, and various men, all leading to this point. She asked them to look at bruises on her body from Ejaz allegedly beating her. The Sergeant asked Detective Webb to look at Leah's body for bruising and marks, as the detective was female. She observed one bruise on Leah. It was faint, an old bruise, located on her back near one side.

Then Leah signed her five-page statement after adding a few sentences, agreeing by her signature that the information contained in the statement was accurate and true. She listed Larry, her "ex husband," as an emergency contact. "I was afraid for my life," Leah told them again.

Sergeant Sims and Detective Webb listened to her and nodded, and then they charged her with the murder of Ejaz Ahmad.

---

7    From Homicide Detective Statement, May 5, 2003, as typed by Elisha Irby 2897, Memphis Police Department.

# CHAPTER 39

Not far from where Leah was confessing, Yared Tedesse was speaking with an investigator. He told of going to the auto auction, about a man named Carlos who took advantage of Ejaz, and about Leah's response when Yared had asked about his friend.

"Who is this 'Carlos'?" The investigator asked him. "What is his last name?"

"I do not know," Yared told him. "Perhaps my friend, Khalifa, knows. He has taken over my shop. I will stop by the shop and ask him when I leave here."

"Where is the shop?"

"On Summer Street."

Later in the day, the investigator's phone rang. It was Yared's voice on the line. "I am at the shop, on Summer."

"Yes."

"My friend Khalifa, he said he does not know Carlos' last name. My friend tells me Carlos is in jail," Yared told the officer politely. "Perhaps I have a number at home. I will call you with it, if I do."

"Yes, thank you."

Johnny Smith tried calling the mosque to ask about his friend. After a few rings, a recording came on. The recorded message asked the caller to remember Ejaz Ahmad, since his untimely death – then someone picked up the receiver and answered the phone.

"Hey, what was that message about Ejaz?" he asked, frantically.

"Oh, no, no, no, no, I cannot say more," said the voice on the other end of the line.

"I heard it!" Johnny demanded. "What was that message about Ejaz?"

After he dropped the phone in its cradle, Johnny sat there in numb shock, until his heart confirmed to him what had happened: *Leah killed Ejaz.*

Jordan had a dream that his father was standing in front of him, smiling gently. Ejaz wore a suit of brilliant white. Jordan looked down and saw that they were standing in white, soft sand. Somehow the dream temporarily made him feel better. It would take a long time before the shock of what happened to his father would wear off.

When a Muslim dies, certain expenses must be taken care of before their Last Will and Testament, the portion containing their final bequests, called a *wasiyya*, can be executed. First to be satisfied is the payment of their debts, funeral expenses, and the distribution of remaining estate, all before the execution of the *wasiyya*. As in all religions, adult Muslims have the legal right to have a will drawn up and their last wishes be made.

Investigators did what they could to assist the family in giving Ejaz as close to a traditional burial as possible by making the autopsy a priority and expediting the process of paperwork being moved through the system so the remains could be released.

Three days after his body was discovered, the Medical Examiner's offices released the remains to family, whereupon Ernestine and Bonnie signed the documents to release Ejaz's to the Muslim community for funeral preparation.

Ejaz was not able to receive a complete Muslim burial with full Islamic customs. It is tradition to close the eyes, bind the jaw, and cover the body with a clean sheet after death. Prior to the funeral, a Muslim of the same sex performs a cleaning ritual of the body. To wrap the body, three white sheets and four ropes are utilized to wrap, right side first, each sheet over the body. One rope secures the wrapping over the head, another just below the feet, and the two remaining used where necessary to secure the sheets. *Salatul Janazah*, a prayer ritual, occurs immediately afterward. The funeral is to take place within twenty-four hours after death. *Hidaad* is the mourning period of three days where crying is allowed, but not loud cries or wailing as it is believed the spirit can hear. The spouse of the deceased is restricted to their home unless they must go out for work or an important errand. During this time of restriction, women cannot wear perfume or jewelry. This phase of mourning, *Iddah*, lasts four months and ten days.

There are prayers at the funeral with men, women, and children assigned designated roles. The funeral procession and the burial have certain traditions to be followed, to include the proper way to mourn and how the body must be placed in the grave. No elaborate markers are used, and no cut flowers, gifts, or candles should be placed on the simple grave. This would be a sign the person's demise was being celebrated, and not their life.

Ejaz's funeral, replete with traditional Islamic prayers and rituals, was very well-attended; so many people came to give their last respects to a man loved by so many. Bonnie asked for a moment alone with his closed casket, and she whispered to Ejaz, her trembling hand laid across the wood. She felt his presence still, and he had come to her in dreams. At times it seemed so surreal, to think of Ejaz's body lying motionless in that box, because he still resided, lively and smiling, in so many hearts.

Ernestine was astounded when she observed over a hundred Muslim men, in the tradition of their faith, all bow in unison at the coffin. Then she saw their faces. They were all crying, grieving for the loss of Ejaz Ahmad.

# CHAPTER 40

*"If anyone I use to ever want to hurt,
it wasn't anyone but me."*
*-Letter from Leah Joy Ward to Judge
Beasley, September 1, 2005*

Leah had made a confession, but the investigation was far from over. Questions had to be answered, evidence had to be gathered and processed, and then it was time to prepare the case for court.

On May 6, the phone rang on the investigator's desk as he was busily scribbling notes to himself.

"I have information on that murder, that murder by Leah Ward," the voice on the line told the investigator.

"Can I ask your name?" The investigator's pencil was poised over a notepad.

"Never mind that." The voice sounded like an African American, definitely male. "I talked to Leah a few days ago and she had told me she and Ejaz were moving closer to the mosque. She didn't want to move there. She was thinking about a divorce, she said. And I saw her when she moved all of that stuff out of their house."

"On Sea Isle?"

"Yeah." The anonymous called continued. "She had a couple o' black guys helping her."

"How many guys?"

"Maybe four, five. And there was this blue car in the yard, a little blue convertible with nice rims, temporary tag. Like the kind you get when you buy a car? Somebody in a van pushed that car out of there.

"I didn't really think of it, you know, at the time. He had a lot o' cars, you know. Then I heard about that murder. And I saw that car again."

"Where at?" The investigator was scribbling furiously, the pencil making scratching noises on the paper.

"At Piggly Wiggly." The caller gave an address for the Piggly Wiggly grocery store. Then he hung up.

Officers arrived at the Piggly Wiggly, a grocery store chain established in 1916, with roots running deep in southern history, recognizable by their mascot, a cheerful pig wearing a butcher's hat. Officers were shopping for something else besides groceries; they were on the lookout for yet another car owned by Ejaz Ahmad.

Parked in the lot near the big, smiling pig logo was a dark blue 1991 Mercury Capri convertible. The car was not in the best shape, quite battered, but it had nice rims. There were no tags.

The officers found a parking sticker for Southwest Tennessee Community College on the window. The driver's side window was down, and it looked like someone either lived in the car or was very messy, for trash was strewn all over the inside.

Nearby on the ground next to the car was a temporary tag issued from the Vance shop where Ejaz's friend worked. "It expires on May 17, this year," an investigator told his partner.

"Let's keep that tag," he was told. The investigator copied down the VIN number and called someone at the office.

"That's not registered," the investigator was told. "But then it doesn't seem like of lot of Ahmad's cars were registered."

The investigator then phoned for a tow truck, and they watched the truck arrive, brakes creaking as it pulled up to the Capri. The car was towed to the vehicle impound lot for processing.

While Ejaz's family and neighbors were being interviewed on May 7, Lieutenant Walter Norris wheeled his car to Vance Road to pick up the car titles to Ejaz's vehicles.

Walid Salam met Norris and welcomed him into the

shop. It smelled like most other repair and auto sales shops: grease, oil, dirt, and cleaner. He went through the receipts and handed Norris several slips of paper bearing the seal of Tennessee. "This is for the white 1995 Mirage," Walid handed him the document. "It is out there, on the lot. It is the car I bought from Ejaz's wife. Here, this one is for the 1996 Hyundai. It is brown."

"Is it here on the lot?" Norris asked, scanning the paperwork.

"Yes," Walid nodded. He returned to the papers in his hand. "There is a 1989 Ford Taurus, a brown wagon, also on the lot."

"Thank you," Norris added it to the stack.

"And this," Walid handed over the title and bill of sale for a 1983 two door Porsche, "but this car is at Compact Auto, which is on Macon Street." The last piece of paperwork was for a 1991 Mercury. "It is on the wrecker," he explained.

Norris ensured he had the bills of sale and titles to all five vehicles. "Can I have a look at that white Mirage that Ejaz's wife drove?"

"Yes sir, of course." Walid stood and walked around the desk. He was going to assist in any way he could. He sorely missed his friend.

Norris retrieved a Polaroid camera from the front seat of his car, and then joined Walid as they strolled over to the white 1995 Mitsubishi Mirage two door. Walid left the investigator to his work.

Norris walked slowly around the vehicle, noting a swipe of blue paint alongside the passenger side of the car. After a few slow steps around, Norris opened the passenger side door, bending to peer closely at the inside of the door, into the lock mechanism, and around the edges. He knelt to get a better look at something that caught his eye: there appeared to be blood on the passenger side floor, on the plastic runner alongside the carpet near the back of the passenger seat. There were also a few hairs trapped in the dried blood. It was not easy to see, but his trained eyes caught it.

Without touching the potential evidence, Norris observed what he thought might possibly be more blood on the back of the passenger seat and on the interior door panel of the same side.

Using his camera, Norris photographed the door, seat, and floor of the vehicle. The camera's flash bounced off the vehicle's interior five times. Norris then made a call to crime scene officers. "I need you to get some possible blood samples, and to lift the hair, from this car," he explained. "If it does test positive for blood, please get me some samples."

He walked out to the lot, five Polaroid photos in one hand, the camera in the other, his face showing he was deep in thought. Norris waved to two officers who arrived to complete a tow ticket for the vehicle.

Crime scene officers arrived about thirty minutes later. They set their kits on the ground, slipping on gloves and protective eyewear as Norris briefed them. Then he stepped back to allow them room to work.

The investigators took numerous photographs of the white car, to include the transfer of blue paint along the passenger side. When satisfied they had captured the vehicle, both in whole and in detail, they opened their kits for retrieving the evidence.

When blood or potential blood evidence is wet, it is absorbed with a dry swab. Dry stains, such as those in the car, may be collected with either scraping or using a swab moistened with distilled water. Wet samples must dry prior to being sealed in an evidence bag. The bag should be paper; paper prevents bacterial growth, which destroys the sample.

One of the investigators now swabbed the potential blood, a separate swab for each stain. The areas on the back of the passenger seat and on the interior door panel both tested negative. Two spots on the plastic runner tested positive.

The hairs were lifted carefully and placed inside evidence

containers.

Another spot was noted; this one was on the rear fender alongside the trunk lid. A presumptive blood test also showed positive for this sample.

When satisfied they had conducted all needed tests, the white car was slowly lifted up to the wrecker bed. With the big dually engine revving, the wrecker pulled out slowly into traffic and headed for the vehicle impound lot.

A visit to Storage USA revealed Leah had recently moved her things out of the storage unit into a larger unit. A search warrant had to be obtained to search the storage unit.

The Selmer Police Department is a small department; it employs twenty full-time employees. There are only three divisions: investigations, narcotics, and patrol. Still, they stay busy, for rural Tennessee is rife with its own share of problems. Meth labs stay busy both churning out the cheap drug and doing their best to avoid police. Rural areas are easy places to set up labs because of the expanse of open land, the understaffing of law enforcement, and the demand for the drug that is concocted out of hazardous materials. Each pound of cooked meth produces about six pounds of toxic materials. Plenty of cheap trailers, the kitchen areas appearing to have been hit by a grenade, dot the rural landscape as testimony to the danger.

It was a call of a different sort that rang through the wires of the Selmer, Tennessee Police station on May 8. "I'm Leah Ward's mother," the caller said. "I just heard she was arrested. She's got some stuff here at my house, and she left a car. I want no part of this. Come and get it away from my house."

When Memphis Police investigators heard of this conversation, they slapped one another on the shoulder, hopeful for another break. They had found Ejaz's Lincoln. Even better, they were told the car keys were under the floor mat, and there was a sword in the trunk. According to her mother, Leah had gone up in the family attic for some reason, and while at her parent's home, she had filled several trash bags full of unknown items to throw away.

Investigators asked one another with raised eyebrows: just what would they find in that attic or that Lincoln?

On the same date that the team was preparing to head for Selmer, Lt. Norris and several investigators met with Jerry Harris of the Attorney General's office. They discussed Tennessee Code section 39-13-204, which discusses sentencing for first-degree murder. The defendant is entitled to a jury trial; if found guilty, the defendant will be sentenced in a separate hearing. The prosecution has to prove an aggravating factor for the defendant to receive the death penalty or life in prison. There are numerous aggravating factors, to include mutilating a dead body. The decision was made to charge Leah with first-degree murder. Leah was facing the death penalty or a life sentence.

Death row housing for women is located at the Tennessee Prison for Women in Nashville. It is in a lockdown area on a housing unit. Across the nation, women account for only one in sixty-seven persons on death row. As of 1900, Tennessee has not executed a woman. Would Leah soon become a resident of this unit, a statistic on executed women?

Five days after Leah made her confession, investigators arrived in Selmer and met with Leah's mother. They took photographs of the Lincoln before the tow truck winched it up, secured the car, and headed for Memphis. Leah's mother signed the Consent to Search. She had the same curling handwriting style as her daughter.

The investigators spoke to Leah's mother briefly; she was cooperative. They searched the attic and around the home. Nothing of evidentiary value was located. Thanking the family, the investigators departed west to Memphis, a two-hour trip on rural roads.

On May 13, The Memphis Police Homicide unit sent the evidence to the Tennessee Bureau of Investigations, located in Nashville. The evidence included blood scrapings from the victim's hand, the victim's hair, the skin removed from the floor of the shed, and an FTA card, which is used to collect, transport, and store DNA samplings. The officers requested comparison testing on the blood evidence to the sample. Officers also requested the TBI identify the type of bullet used to kill the victim.

Walid Salam spoke to Memphis Police homicide investigator Sergeant Fitzpatrick about Walid's relationship with Ejaz, meeting Fitzpatrick at an office on Poplar Street on May 17th at about 1:00 p.m.

Walid explained politely that he had known Ejaz for a year or so. He spoke of their dealings with Regal Imports and Vance Avenue. He recalled the incident at the restaurant, Spaghetti Factory, when Leah screamingly accused Ejaz of cheating on her with Walid's secretary. It was the only time he had any dealings with Leah, he told Sergeant Fitzpatrick, until she showed up on April 28th to sell the white Mitsubishi Mirage. Walid detailed the next three days he spent dealing with Leah about vehicles. He also told Sergeant Fitzpatrick about that horrible smell. And yes, Leah had told Walid that Ejaz was in Pakistan, he confirmed when asked.

"I was just trying to help her out," Walid Salam told the investigator.

Investigators still had much to do to make their case. On May 21, 2003, an affidavit for a subpoena was drawn up to obtain copies of Leah's fingerprint and the pawn ticket. A photo was made of the pawned ring.

Officers obtained copies of both the truck rental agreement and the storage unit agreement Leah had signed. The paperwork from Storage USA confirmed Leah had rented a moving truck and a storage space. The 10' by 15' storage unit was pre-paid for a six-month lease, the same amount of time Leah thought she would be serving her sentence. For whatever reason, she had paid a bit over the charge for renting the storage unit. Officers noted the alternative contact "Jane Doe, phone number 555-1212," and shook their heads. "555" was a prefix often used in television and movies because it did not actually exist. "Jane Doe"? They looked skeptically at one another over the copy sheets of paper.

Leah Joy Ward was finally scheduled to make an appearance for her arraignment. When she walked into the courtroom, those in the gallery had to keep from gasping aloud.

She had shaved off all of her long, blonde hair, her head shorn to the scalp. She was considerably heavier; the starch-heavy jailhouse chow had added some pounds on her small frame. "She was only 27 years old," said an observer, "but she looked 45." Leah's antics also caught everyone's attention.

As the judge began proceedings, Leah sank to the floor. She curled up in a fetal position, remained that way for the entire arraignment hearing.

Johnny Smith missed his good friend terribly, and he was filled with rage at Leah. He told a friend about a dream he had several days after he discovered Ejaz was murdered. He dreamed he was asleep on his mat in Ejaz's guest room. Something woke him and he got up. The house was eerily quiet. The furniture, rugs, and pictures were gone. There were shards of glass and litter on the floors. Johnny walked slowly into the living room, where he saw a television set. It was turned on, but the picture was badly out of focus, snowy, flickering on the screen. Then he woke up, shaking.

About 3:30 p.m. on May 17, 2003, Ernestine Marsh, Bonnie, and Jordan met Memphis Police homicide investigator Sergeant James Fitzpatrick at the Sea Isle home. None of Ejaz's family or friends had a key to his house. A locksmith had been called, and he arrived and opened the front door to Ejaz's home.

Fitzpatrick had asked Ernestine and Bonnie to accompany him on a walk-through of the brick home to examine the premises, in case the crime scene investigators had missed anything deemed pertinent to the investigation. Hearts still aching, the women and the little boy walked through the residence. They each explained to the investigator how so many items were missing, to include Ejaz's collection of numerous swords. "The police needs to get them for testing," Ernestine told Fitzpatrick.

Fitzpatrick explained to them that swords had been located in the storage unit. "At this point the items in that storage unit aren't pertinent to the investigation," he explained.

The trash remained scattered about on the carport, refuse dumped when Leah had cleared the house of belongings. Ernestine walked around the carport, studying those remnants of Leah's life with Ejaz, Evidently it all had been worthless to Leah for she did not store or take it with her. The Memphis area thunderstorms of early May had soaked the debris, and the mud had left a layer of dirt over much of the items. Ernestine sifted through the damp mess. She found a used woman's wallet. Out of curiosity, she opened the wallet. Bonnie's old driver's license was in the wallet. Ernestine held onto the license, wondering, why would Leah have kept anything related to Bonnie?

She looked through the bags of trash on the porch, and came across several syrupy greeting cards addressed to Ejaz, now covered in dirt. "I love you," Leah had signed them. In one of the bags, Ernestine found pictures of Jordan. It looked like Leah had just gathered up all evidence of Ejaz's life – photos, mementoes, cards, notes, and business papers – and dumped it all in garbage bags as trash.

Ernestine stepped to the backyard and observed a pan that was lying in the yard. Ernestine's police experience came back to her, as she could tell this pan "had been used to cook crystal meth."

Ernestine slipped through the back door, her heart aching. She walked through the silent, empty rooms, wondering what exactly Ejaz had gone though. As painful and frightening as it was, she simply had to, as best she could, reenact Leah's steps that day.

Ernestine walked to the closet where, according to Jordan, the gun had been stashed on a top shelf. Ernestine, knowing she was a few inches taller than Leah, reached up into the closet, her hand as far as she could stretch, but she still could not reach the shelf. She retrieved a chair to stand on, stepped up, and only then could she reach the shelf. She began to see it all in her mind. If the gun was hidden where Jordan told her, then Leah could not have just reached up to retrieve it. To Ernestine, this meant premeditation.

The closet that held the antiques, expensive rugs, and items from Pakistan was now empty. The tasteful furnishings throughout the home, including the expensive rugs, were gone.

The bathroom area still reeked. From her days as an investigator, Ernestine knew it was the smell of death.

She found Leah's makeup case in a cloth bag on a bathroom shelf. There were several shell casings from spent bullets in the little cloth bag. Near the washer and dryer, Ernestine found some Amway brand cleaner. It made Ernestine remember how excited Ejaz had been when he told her his next business venture would be to sell Amway.

She opened the lid to the washing machine. The clothes in there were dried from having been in there for some time. Ernestine pulled out Leah's work uniform, then Ejaz's white sherwani and kurta.[8] Both bore the sour smell of clothing that had dried slowly in a closed washing machine.

Something told her to look in the refrigerator, and when she did, what she saw in the freezer made her reel back. A set of teeth, belonging to a head in a frozen bag, grinned menacingly back at her. It took her a second to realize it was a frozen goat's head. Ernestine, in tears, slammed the freezer door.

She returned Bonnie's driver's license to her, as she told

8   The sherwani is a long sleeved jacket that hangs to mid-calf; kurtas are the pants worn under the coat. Both are usually formal wear.

her the story about finding it in the wallet on Ejaz's carport. "It's your old one, with the address of where you used to live."

"I know why he had this," Bonnie told her mother. "Ejaz was doing my taxes for me, and I gave him the license for information. But why would it be in Leah's wallet?" Unfortunately, at a later date when she checked her credit, she had her answer. Leah had used Bonnie's old license to obtain credit cards, which were promptly maxed out but never paid. Bonnie never received bills or notices because the accounts had been opened using her old address.

It would take years to repair her credit score. It would take longer to recover emotionally.

Bonnie also made the trek through Ejaz's home. She was hoping to salvage some mementos for Jordan and Drake.

On the floor of Ejaz's bedroom, Bonnie found a photo of Ejaz and baby Jordan, along with a pair of Ejaz's eyeglasses. She walked through the eerie house. She pushed piles of debris and refuse aside with her foot, and in so doing, managed to salvage a few more photographs.

*She just dumped it all,* Bonnie told herself. *Didn't she care? How could she not care? Ejaz did so much for her! She claimed she cared for Jordan. What a lying bitch ... all lies, so many lies.* As Bonnie walked out of the house, arms folded tightly, tears in her eyes, she wondered, *now that she's in jail, what will she do? What lies will she tell now?*

From her cell in the Memphis jail, Leah began to send letters and handwritten legal documents to the court. In prison world jargon, Leah became a "paper hanger" and a "jailhouse lawyer."

"Paperhangers" file motions about anything and everything they deem unfair. "I have seen inmates file complaints and try to sue anyone for anything," said one seasoned correctional officer. "Because they received two less green beans on their plate than the other inmates. Because a dead bird was on the prison grounds. One inmate even tried to sue me because I told him to stop blocking the door and to allow inmates in wheelchairs to roll through."

"Jailhouse lawyers" are inmates who assist inmates in doing legal paperwork, although they generally begin by learning in order to help themselves. Sometimes they have experience in the field, but more frequently, they are self-taught. Other inmates will pay, usually in commissary items, to have the jailhouse lawyer help them to file their paperwork. Often jailhouse lawyers become quite skilled in what they are doing, and their work can be as good as any paralegal's.

While incarcerated in Jail East, Leah had a physical fight with another female inmate. She later claimed she fought in self-defense because the woman was demanding sex. As a result, Leah was placed in an area called "F Pod." Typical of Leah, she felt it was unfair and did not understand why she was punished for fighting when she was not the aggressor.

# CHAPTER 41

*"I know probably each day you hear lies by people that committed a crime and swear they didn't do it ..."*
*- Letter from Leah Ward to Judge Beasley, September 12, 2005*

The Grand Jury met during the May term of 2003. They determined there was sufficient evidence to charge Leah Ward: "Between April 1, 2003 and May 2, 2003 ... (Ward) did unlawfully, intentionally, and with premeditation kill Ejaz Ahmad...." The net tightened around Leah. Pulling those ropes were two brilliant prosecutors in the district attorney's offices.

Pamela Fleming was waiting for the elevator in the Shelby County Justice Center when it stopped and the doors creaked open. A few people exited, holding the elevator door open for one another. As they all parted ways, Pamela saw Assistant District Attorney Patience "Missy" Branham standing in the elevator.

Pamela had just completed her internship in the D.A.'s office, and was now moving to her new office upstairs. She was about to greet Missy when the Assistant D.A. called out to her, "What Division are you in now?"

Pamela blinked, taken aback. "Uh ... ten."

"Good!" Missy said. "Want to assist on a murder case?"

As the elevator doors were closing, Pamela shouted to Missy, "Sure!" Pamela was trying not to appear shocked, but "my eyes were big as saucers," she later laughed. "I was a baby – I mean, a *baby* – attorney and this was to be my first jury trial." As a result, Pamela Fleming became the assistant prosecutor for State of Tennessee vs. Leah Joy Ward.

Walking back to her new office, Pamela Fleming felt a strange sensation between fear and excitement. It was not unlike the fear and excitement for previous challenges she faced up to this time in her career.

The child of military parents, Pamela was born in the Army base hospital at Fort Benning, Georgia. She considers herself from "everywhere," as the family moved where the Army needed her parents most. At seventeen, Pamela dropped out of high school and immediately obtained her G.E.D. In January 1992, she entered the doors of Jackson State Community College.

As the first community college in West Tennessee, it had been established in 1967. Pamela Fleming was the first person in her family to obtain a college diploma when she strode across the graduation ceremony's stage to receive her associate degree.

She was a sharp girl, and knew she needed to prove to herself and her family that she could do something better with her life by continuing to pursue a college degree.

She received a full scholarship to the University of Tennessee in Martin. After receiving her bachelor's degree in Criminal Justice, she took the LSAT with her sights on law school. Like so many potential law students, Pamela felt doubt nibbling as she completed the application process. "What if I don't get accepted?" she worried, considering what she wanted as a backup plan. So she began work on a Masters Degree in Criminology. While working on the Masters, she took the LSAT with another group of hopeful students. She made the highest score in the group. Pamela was going to law school.

During her collegiate career, she became a single mom raising her three children. They were part of her reason to go far, to reach goals.

Still working on the Criminology degree, she began classes at the esteemed Cecil C. Humphreys School of Law in Memphis, Tennessee. As the only law school in Memphis, and one of the largest in the state, the school set the bar high and demanded only the best from its students, and Pamela

Fleming delivered. Her hard work paid off, and she was made an offer

"We will cover your tuition one hundred percent," she was told, "plus a stipend, if you will agree to teach after graduation."

Accepting the offer, she again felt a strange sensation between fear and excitement. "Hey, pay me to go to law school with a free education?" She could not help but grin widely. "Not bad for a high school dropout, single mom, with three kids!"

Still in grad school, Pamela found studies easy, because she loved the debates of theory and being able to utilize creativity with her work. Law School, however, was no comparison. She felt that, sometimes, she knew nothing at all, despite a quality education and stellar grades. She managed to find a balance in working simultaneously on the two degrees. Meanwhile, she was working and raising her children.

A reprimand from an esteemed professor didn't help to encourage her. "You'll never be a trial attorney," the older woman promised Pamela, "because you don't attend moot court."

"I have three kids, working on two degrees, *and* going to work," Pamela explained. "I don't have *any* time for anything, including moot court."

"Well," the professor sniffed, "you won't make it." The professor's words rang in her ear, and they stung.

Later, after over a hundred trial cases in her successful career, Pamela Fleming sometimes considers picking up the phone and asking that professor, "So, how is moot court?"

Judge James C. Beasley, Jr., is the judge of Division 10 in the 30th Judicial District of Shelby County. He sports a wide smile, silver-framed eyeglasses, and a bald head encircled by short, graying hair. The criminal court judge contributes articles to various publications, to include the *Memphis Flyer*. Judge Beasley received his undergraduate degree in 1993; his law degree was obtained at Memphis State University. Judge Beasley was a member of the Shelby County Bar Association, the Tennessee Judicial Conference, and the Tennessee Trial Judges Conference. He was appointed to Criminal Court, Division 10 in 1995 after serving as the Assistant District Attorney General. Now he was overseeing The State of Tennessee vs. Leah Joy Ward.

It would be a case none of them could forget. Leah Ward herself made sure of that.

# CHAPTER 42

A court order of August 25, 2004, ordered the Sheriff's Department to transfer Leah to Memphis Mental Health Institute (MMHI) for a mental health evaluation prior to her trial, to ensure she was competent to stand trial. Leah was transported on the same day the order was signed. The escorting officers, along with their charge, arrived at MMHI, and signed her over according to the paperwork for the in-patient forensic examination. Leah was admitted and became a ward of the MMHI.

One of the mandatory tests given to female patients upon admission to MMHI is a pregnancy test, and Leah's results were negative.

She was assigned a room with three other women, and was briefed on the rules and expectations, as well as careful instruction on what constituted proper behavior.

Despite having been given specific instruction, Leah had to be told by staff members, on more than one occasion, to stop behaving in certain ways with some of the male patients. At one point she was observed, "French kissing" a male patient.

While at MMHI, Leah became friends with a handsome, black male patient named D'wayne Curb. D'wayne was also a jail inmate who had been sent to MMHI for an evaluation.

D'wayne Curb had left a wife, child, and parole officer in Memphis as well as a rap sheet that ran for many pages. His criminal history report listed misdemeanors such as contributing to the delinquency of a minor, disturbing the peace, running a red light, theft of property under $500, driving without a vehicle registration, a valid operator's license, or insurance; reckless driving, driving while under the influence, and public intoxication. Not all of his crimes were so petty. D'wayne had numerous felony arrests for crimes such as possession of cocaine with intent to distribute, possession of a handgun as a convicted felon, aggravated robbery, parole violation, burglary, and larceny. His rap sheet also listed numerous aliases he had used. This violent and habitual criminal's life was about to become even more complicated when he met Leah Joy Ward.

D'wayne spent a lot of time watching television in the day room. He also slept, trying to pass the days. He noted staff members rushing into the room of a patient named Leah when Leah was hitting her head against the walls or screaming and out of control. He talked with Leah on occasion, just like anyone else, but she had a penchant for cursing out patients so he remained a casual acquaintance. They spoke on occasion.

Leah told him that "someone," a patient, was bothering her. D'wayne was a part of the legal system's revolving door, already very familiar with inmate and patient complaints and chatter so he ignored this complaint.

D'wayne did not join anyone, including Leah Ward, for cigarette breaks. "I don't smoke," he told them, when asked, "I hate cigarettes."

Prior to D'wayne's hospital release, Leah had a request, stating she dearly needed him to bring her some nail polish and makeup.

D'wayne was discharged from the hospital in mid-October. That following day, he walked out of jail on a discharge. He went to visit Leah and a few other patients at MMHI that evening. He gave Leah a hug and kissed her on her cheek, "a normal thing to do," he later explained to investigators. Just as they settled in for a visit, Leah asked him about her nail polish and makeup, but before he could answer her, security arrived to escort him out. He was not supposed to visit, they explained. "You can't visit until you have been released for six months," he was told.

"I didn't know," D'wayne told them, and left the building without incident. He did not enjoy freedom for long. D'wayne was arrested on a warrant on October 15, 2004.

Leah was officially deemed competent for trial. Officers arrived, signed the necessary documentation, and departed with Leah, now in their official custody. She was returned to the jail on October 15, 2004.

That next day, an officer in the jail advised a supervisor that Leah was reporting a sexual assault. The supervisor made arrangements for officers to transport Leah to the Memphis Sexual Assault Resource Center. Per protocol, Leah was transferred to MSARC via a law enforcement vehicle. Through the window, as they rolled through the city, she was able to watch Memphis' famous Union Avenue float past.

Then the jail supervisor's phone rang again.

An MSARC nurse performed a pregnancy test on Leah; it was positive. "The nurse says she needs an ultrasound to see how far along she is," the officer explained to the supervisor.

Leah Ward was returned to the jail as an expectant mother.

Two female law enforcement investigators arrived on October 18 to interview the pregnant inmate about the alleged rape. It meant another chapter in the saga of Leah Joy Ward.

Leah was carefully interviewed, with no demands, with gentle voices and slow questioning tactics. The investigators assured her she was safe and part of their job was to ensure no one else was assaulted. It was not the officer's goals to interrogate or judge her; only to obtain the case facts and assure her it was safe to report.

Interviewing her proved to be difficult as she gave partial and conflicting answers. She told them she was afraid, so she could not remember details. Sometimes she spoke in confusing sentences.

Leah reported she had been incarcerated in Jail East since September 3, 2003. She could not recall why she was sent to the Memphis Mental Health Center. She could not name her attorney or the judge who signed the court order. She could describe the MMHC doctor who oversaw her case, but did not recall the name of the doctor until the officers asked, "Was it doctor ___?"

Leah told the investigators the doctor only laughed at her when she tried to speak with him. She told the investigators that when she tried to talk to hospital staff, they would "shoot (her) up" with medication.

The investigators moved gently into questions regarding the alleged rape. Leah told them she was afraid to report her attacker's name, because staff at MMHC "hurt" people at the Center. Her tears flowed as she explained one of her friends, a man named Will, was often beaten for not being quiet. One of the three women who shared a room with Leah, a woman who remained at MMHC, was also beaten for causing trouble. "Them people out there don't listen," she said of the MMHC staff.

She was scared, she told them, because "that guy that stuck his dick in me said he's got a machine gun." Then she moved from being afraid to name her attacker to saying his name. She named this alleged rapist as a patient named D'wayne Curb. She described his room's proximity to hers at the hospital, explaining he had a room on the same hallway where she was assigned, but "a long way away" from the hall where her room was located.

Room doors remained unlocked, Leah explained; this allowed many men to come into her room demanding sex. She did not like it when they would give her strange looks, but she did not want these people to get into trouble so she did not want to admit who they were.

In halting words, Leah told of a male staff member who came into her room at night demanding sex, and explained that this male staff member assaulted her in a common area. She admitted that she was breaking a rule for being in this area without a supervisor. She then said he was a supervisor, but she was afraid of getting in trouble so she complied. She thought the assault occurred at daytime, and then she was sure it happened during the night.

She insisted D'wayne did not come into her room, but she did not recall who did walk in.

Leah told the investigators she was sitting in a common room when D'wayne sexually assaulted her.

Leah told them, in her expressionless voice, that she had tried to be just friends with D'wayne, but he kept bothering her. He followed her around, standing in lines behind her, bossing her around, touching her inappropriately, and being a nuisance. She tried talking to him, and even yelling at him, to leave her alone. According to Leah, she complained, but to no avail, saying that both staff and patients told her to simmer down, and the doctor had just laughed in her face.

Then she changed her story and told investigators that yes, D'wayne did come into her room. Then she corrected herself, saying he would show up at the door, and that even her roommates yelled at him to leave.

Leah rambled to the investigators that she had been in MMHC only a few days when she wandered into a dark room, and then she was on the floor in this dark room. The investigators asked her how and why she entered this room. They asked her for specifics about the room, its location, its use. Was it a supply closet? Leah couldn't remember.

Then Leah guessed that D'wayne had told her to meet him there. D'wayne was standing next to an open doorway of a room and told her "come here." Leah entered the room and the door was closed behind her; it was too dark to see. She knew D'wayne was in the room along with someone else, a man, but it was too dark to identify this second man; he never spoke so she did not recognize a voice.

Leah thought she may be in a supply room, but it was so "pitch dark black" she could not figure out where she was. She knew it was not a bedroom. D'wayne assaulted her in this room, the other man watching, but she was afraid to say anything because of the other man.

She asked the interviewers for a definition of "willingly."

She was unsure if she had sex willingly, as she did not scream but it did not feel right.

After the alleged sexual assault by D'wayne in the dark room, she said she had requested a bath, claiming that she felt so dirty that she felt suicidal. In doing so, she had tried to drown herself, by flooding the bathtub, which ended up flooding the room. Leah said that she was in trouble for doing it, but she still could not bring herself to report the assault to hospital staff.

Leah explained haltingly how a male staff member came into her bathroom at night to assault her.

She also told of another alleged assault committed by a second staff member, this time a muscular male who wore a uniform, and sometimes he wore "street" clothes while working. He was a sharp dresser, she recalled. This man came into her room during the day to assault her while she was in the bathroom. This time, a nurse walked in, told them to stop what they were doing, and walked out. Leah did not give details about what he was doing to her or what the nurse observed.

She claimed to be unsure of the meaning of the word "ejaculate." She asked the investigators if it meant, "to come." She claimed she did not want to say certain words because they were not "nice" words. The investigators assured her language was not a problem. They only wanted the truth.

All total, Leah reported sexual assault by three employees and one patient. She tried to report the assaults while in the hospital, she claimed, but hospital staff would laugh at her in disbelief. She felt no one believed or cared about her, despite numerous attempts for help. She feared being physically harmed by staff. She was hearing voices in her head; sometimes, she felt the sexual assaults were all her fault. Sometimes it all seemed like a dream. Her fears were causing her to have insomnia.

Leah told them she was certain D'wayne was the father

of her unborn child. She had no doubts. She felt she was pregnant when she missed her period and was nauseated and the test confirmed her suspicions.

The investigators completed incident reports and lengthy, detailed reports about the interview. The investigators worked with officials outside of the department, sharing information and discussing the case, spending many collective hours on the case to ensure all information was correct and properly documented.

That same week, a Tennessee Mental Health Investigator, Mr. David Abers, interviewed Leah.

Leah told Dr. Abers that she remembered now that a staff member had unlocked the door to a storage closet to allow D'wayne and herself inside, possibly to smoke cigarettes. Instead, D'wayne raped her. When she left the closet, the same staff member walked her back to her room while making sexual comments.

Leah explained she only had sexual contact with D'wayne while at MMHC. During the entire interview with Dr. Abers, Leah never reported sexual misconduct by staff.

Dr. Abers asked her if she were sexually active and she denied it. She had not been sexually active nor was she sexually assaulted while at Jail East, Leah explained. She admitted she did get into an altercation with another female inmate, a woman who demanded sex, she told the doctor. Now she was in F Pod, but she had no idea why.

On October 21, 2004, the female law enforcement investigators returned to interview Leah a second time; she was visiting with her attorney, so the investigators could not conduct an interview.

The following day, a physician saw Leah because she had an ear infection. She had stuffed tissues in both ears, perhaps as a way to shut out the jail noises. Stuffing the tissues into her ear canal had caused the infection.

In late October, investigators were able to interview D'wayne Curb. It was easy to locate him; D'wayne was locked up in the county jail, having been picked up for an outstanding warrant for a failure to appear. "Nobody told me I had a court date," he told the officers. It seemed D'wayne could not stay out of trouble. He was bounced back into the legal system.

On October 28, Mr. David Abers, the investigator with Tennessee Mental Health, interviewed D'wayne. The following day, D'wayne was again taken out of his cell, this time to meet with law enforcement investigators regarding the allegations of rape.

D'wayne admitted he had casual conversation with Leah Ward, who he identified in a photo, as it was the norm to chitchat with other patients. He denied ever sexually assaulting anyone, but could only say that he didn't "think" he had sex with Leah while housed at MMHI. Later in the interview, he was adamant there were no sexual advances, certainly not intercourse of any kind. He did not recall meeting her in a closet. He told investigators male staff did go into her room, but only when she was "having fits." She was restrained at least once due to her behavior; it was male staff that had to restrain her. Rumor had it they had doped her up with a shot, but D'wayne paid no heed to gossip.

He was not aware of her pregnancy until investigators shared the information.

# CHAPTER 43

The cold Tennessee winter winds of February whipped around Memphis street corners as the second month of the New Year began. As 2004 had rolled away, Leah was anticipating the arrival of her baby. She was transported to the UT Medical Group in Germantown, Tennessee, and a Pregnancy Record was completed. The form also requested information regarding "mental" disorders; her last psychiatric evaluation was noted as October 2004. Because she was pregnant, all of her psychiatric medications, Prozac, Paxil, Trazadone, and Risperdal, had been stopped. An infection screening revealed she had a sexually transmitted disease. She filled in on the form that she had two living children and had had two spontaneous abortions (miscarriages).

On March 14, 2005, Leah filed a complaint against Shelby County alleging that she was raped while at the Memphis Mental Health Institute. Shelby County filed to dismiss the case based on the fact she was not raped while under the custody of a Shelby County Sheriff's officer. Therefore, the office could not be held legally liable. There were no Shelby County jail personnel present at the time of the rape, and MMHI is not part of the Shelby County government. Shelby County's request for dismissal of the case was granted.

Several trial dates were set, and then changed. One of Leah's attorneys had to have surgery, so the trial date was moved forward. By the time the attorney was ready to return, Leah was almost eight months pregnant with the child she claimed to be the result of her rape. The prosecution asked the date be forwarded again, as they did not want to place a pregnant woman on the stand. A pregnant woman on the stand, regardless of what she is accused of, affects the juries by garnering sympathy. And, if Leah were to have the baby during trial, it would interrupt not just the flow of the trial, but cost additional money and time. Besides, the stress and physical demands may cause problems in the pregnancy. No one wanted that.

In mid-April of 2005, Leah sat down once again to pen a letter to Judge Beasley. She was eight months pregnant, due to deliver in about six weeks. As she wrote, her brow furrowed; she was concerned the child she carried would become a ward of the state. As she wrote, one hand caressed her swollen belly. She felt a bond with this baby; she wanted a loving family to adopt the baby so it would not become a part of the system, passed from foster care office to foster homes and back again. She asked Judge Beasley for assistance. "Will you please be willing to help me or refer me to someone with an adoptive agency that will be willing to place this child in a loving home to good parents?" she wrote.

On June 20, Leah went into labor while behind the bars of the Shelby County jail. She was rushed to the hospital. She delivered a healthy baby girl in the wee hours of the morning, one hour after she was admitted. She was released from the hospital the next day, and now took the ride back to the jail without her child. It seemed strange and surreal, to not have that familiar movement in a swollen tummy.

Leah was also concerned about her "mental status." She wrote Judge Beasley in early July 2005, "I am seeking to become better," she assured him, and not requesting assistance for her criminal case. She explained how, in Jail East, she had requested help but was locked up in F-Pod 23/1 "caged up like an animal." The move did not help; she only felt worse. She was again being medicated with Paxil, a prescription drug used to treat post-traumatic stress disorder (PTSD), obsessive-compulsive disorder, depression, anxiety disorders, and premenstrual problems. She was upset that doctors at MMHI only tested her for competence to stand trial, and did not diagnose nor treat her symptoms. She understood the loss of her baby to adoption was a part of the melancholy that surrounded her, but she also blamed the "rape" on "hearing voices, I cry a lot, and am very depressed." She did not want to "become suicidal" and was afraid to tell the jail staff because she certainly did not want to return to F-Pod. She asked the Judge to "find someone who can help me."

While Leah was writing to Judge Beasley, the legal case paperwork on the alleged rape was completed, the case carefully reviewed, and a meeting was held with the Attorney Generals. In August 2005, the decision was made to not prosecute, due to a lack of evidence, and Leah was advised of the decision.

On September 1, 2005, Leah wrote a letter to Judge Beasley expressing regret and sorrow over murdering Ejaz. "If anyone I use to ever want to hurt, it wasn't anyone but me," she wrote. "Wether [Sic] I am locked up I know I deserve a sentence of life. I even deserve death, for what I have done." She vacillated between asking for forgiveness and self-blame. "I was already a prisoner while I was free before I was locked up," she wrote.

On September 12, 2005, Leah sent another handwritten letter to Judge Beasley. She was upset that no photographs were taken of her bruises during her confession interview on May 5, as she claimed they were from Ejaz beating her. "I shot him with no intention to kill him," she patiently explained. She admitted to shooting Ejaz but only in self-defense "to save my life to get away from him that was my only way. I tried other ways but I never could get away from him because he overpowered me," she wrote. "I know probably each day you hear lies by people that committed a crime and swear they didn't do it. Each word I speak is the truth. If only there were a machine or something for you to help you believe…" [Sic]

Leah wrote out a Motion for Dismissal on September 22, 2005, requesting her attorneys, Public Defenders Harry Sayle and Sandra Kent, be removed from her case on the grounds of "unethical and inaffective [Sic] assistance of counsel and conflict of interest." She wrote it out by hand in neat print. She then wrote a letter to Judge Beasley explaining she had no communication with her lawyers, and explained if she were not afforded a lawyer, she would represent herself.

In another letter to Judge Beasley dated October 31, 2005, she begged for assistance in prosecuting the alleged rapist. "I wanted to be a mom to my (child) but I was ripped from my rights to parent her because of being incarcerated," she penned in her neat hand. "I want to be a mother to my baby and my other 2 children that I have."

Assistant District Attorneys Missy Branham and Pamela Fleming were adding items to a "to do" list as fast they checked off items. Both women heard about the scene in court when a bald Leah had rolled on the floor of Judge Beasley's courtroom. It was not the strangest thing anyone had done in a Memphis courtroom, but it was, for the time, the most interesting. Leah's behavior remained the scuttlebutt in the justice department for a long time.

"I don't see how she was able to drag a grown dead man into that shed," Pamela told Missy over a conference table, while poring over notes, records, and crime scene photos. She indicated one of the pictures. "See how far the shed is from the back door?"

Missy picked up the photograph and scribbled some notes on a yellow pad of paper. "Let's go out there and see," she said. The address on Sea Isle was written down on their list.

# CHAPTER 44

Missy Branham and Pamela Fleming arrived at the house on Sea Isle. Both were surprised that the house had new occupants so soon. It seemed the entire home would still smell horrific.

"I don't see how they got the smell out of there," Missy shook her head.

"I don't see how anyone had sex in there, when the body was in the bathroom," Pamela shuddered, thinking about the condom that was discovered in the house by crime scene investigators.

"Well, she did tell people that the refrigerator broke and a bunch of meat had spoiled." Missy led the way up the drive.

Ever practical, Pamela grimaced. "*Still.*"

They leaned over the fence to get a good look at the backyard. In reality, the shed was not as far from the back door as it appeared in crime scene photographs.

Pamela thought of how many times she had moved heavy furniture by herself. "You know, the way she had the body wrapped in that plastic; that plastic would have slid easily." She pointed from the back sliding glass door to the shed. "If I want to move something heavy across carpet, I stick a piece of hard plastic under it; if it's on a floor without carpet, I place carpet or plastic under it ... it moves easier."

Missy was nodding, following the same line of sight. "It's doable," she said.

Pamela could picture Leah, possibly high, dragging a body wrapped in plastic across the short expansion of lawn to dump it into the shed. She thought of how an adrenaline rush can help a person move objects they never thought possible, or of how drugs can make a person feel big and bulletproof. "Oh yeah," she agreed, "It's definitely doable."

Both attorneys made an appointment to meet Leah's parents at a diner near their home. They sat in a booth and gently began asking questions and jotting notes. Leah's parents were salt-of-the-earth, middle-class, rural, pious people who spoke casually about their daughter's indiscretions, including being charged with murder.

To one of the attorneys, Leah's parents "seemed to be the type who believed parents owed their adult children nothing: they gave birth, raised them, then cut the ties when their child became an adult, believing that child was on their own, to make their own decisions."

"The first time Leah does something, she always gets caught" one of her parents explained Leah's bad luck.

"It's in all the papers around here," one of Leah's parents said, gesturing to the world outside of the café. They seemed more upset about the negative media coverage than the fact their daughter was being tried for murder. Pamela Fleming later noted, "They were from the 1950s, with middle-class attitudes and old-school beliefs." Still, their blasé attitudes struck Pamela as odd. "Surreal" she would later describe the visit.

Pamela had been taught by detectives to never say, "I've seen it all" because the next case might be even more heinous.

"At one point, we were actually questioning if we could even take it to trial." Pamela Fleming says now. "It was just after 9/11, and public feelings were so harsh towards Muslims, and anyone from the Middle East, that we were unsure if people could be impartial."

Leah did seem sincere about some things, including the wearing of the hijab, even if sporadic. But still, investigators asked one another, did she wear it as a sort of "jab" at her parents, trying to upset her family? Is that why she befriended and began dating African Americans, to shock the conservative community where she grew up? None of it was admissible in a trial, nor did it have any legal bearing on the murder. Still, it provided some insight to help explain Leah Ward's behavior.

Missy and Pamela spent weeks tracking down people who knew, or even might have known, Ejaz Ahmad. They spoke with neighbors, friends, coworkers, and took a drive to the mosque. No matter who or how they asked, the bottom line was always the same: Ejaz was a good person, an educated self-made man who was against drugs, violence, or anything on the wrong side of the law. "The only bad thing we could find," one of the attorneys recalls, "is a criminal trespass in Mississippi," referring to one incident where Ejaz and Bonnie had an argument over the custody of their son Jordan, and Bonnie called the law on Ejaz. There was no physical fighting, just angry words.

"I just don't believe Leah's story," Pamela remarked to Missy. "First of all, it would be so out of character for this man to cheat on a wife." Missy agreed with her.

Pamela shuffled through her notes as she sat in her office, pushing aside files and stacks of papers to jot down notes on a pad of paper. She referred back to her college education, likening Leah's behavior to a person who is emotionally stuck in adolescence. When she reviewed the file and the notes, she could not help but notice how Leah's actions, her thinking patterns, were so juvenile. "She just saw herself as the center of everything. She thinks she can outsmart everyone," Pamela noted. Everything Leah did, it seemed, was manipulation by an egocentric woman who thought she did no wrong, and appeared to be so shortsighted that perhaps she just did not think things through. Pamela glanced through the crime scene photos, the police reports. She and Missy had agreed that Leah was trying to cut up the dead body and scatter the parts so they would never be located. Leah's plan was to tell everyone Ejaz had left her and walked away from the people he loved and the life he had created for himself.

It was also possible that the decapitation was an intentional "jab" at Ejaz and his religion, because Leah knew the requirements for a Muslim burial. Removal of the penis was usually some a crime of retaliation, or perhaps in Leah's case, the lack of ability to control her emotions. Maybe she thought removing the scrotum would make it easier to cut off the legs. None of this could be used in the courtroom, but Pamela Fleming still loved the psychology of crime, to discuss theory.

What did Leah think would happen, being in jail for four months and the smell of death finally leaked through the entire neighborhood? Was she just hoping, or thinking, that she would not be a suspect? Did she even *think*?

Again, with regard to the alleged rape, Leah's story changed, her words molded and shifted in an effort to hide lies. "Do you know what I believe?" Pamela would later ask. "I think she had sex with someone in the jail, found out she was pregnant, so she conjured up that whole 'rape at MMHI' thing before she even was admitted to MMHI."

When it was time to go to court, the team of prosecutors felt ready. Based on the evidence and witness testimonies they had amassed in an effort to prove Leah Joy Ward's guilt beyond a shadow of a doubt, Missy and Pamela felt they had come to know this strange woman.

And they were demanding justice for Ejaz.

# CHAPTER 45

The trial began on Thursday, November 1, 2005, and was covered live. As only one camera was allowed in the courtroom, news stations shared the footage, with reporters in a separate room watching the trial unfold. While it did not always make headlines, there was press in the daily newspapers.

After the birth of her last child, Leah was back on Paxil, which would eventually be changed to Celexa and Hydroxyzine. She sat demurely next to her attorney, her blue eyes skirting the courtroom.

The jury of nine women and three men filed in to take their seats. Some glanced at Leah in interest, while others gazed about the room.

The state opened by explaining to the jury how Ejaz Ahmad was a kind person who wanted to assist others, in part because of his religious values. "He was a victim of his own compassion," Missy told them.

It was pointed out that Ejaz's friends felt the defendant was "possessive and controlling." Missy Branham gave a short narrative of events, from Ejaz giving Leah his own home while he moved out, to his decomposed body discovered in the shed by his then eleven-year-old son. Despite Leah's insistence that Ejaz had broken down doors and windows in efforts to attack her, the home showed no such damage. After Ejaz's death, Leah stole or sold everything, packing up what remained to store in a storage warehouse.

Public Defender Kathy Kent explained there was no doubt Leah did fire the gun that took Ejaz's life, but it was in self defense from an angry, abusive man who was actively attacking Leah, and Leah feared for her life. Intelligent and good at detail, the attorney patiently discussed Leah's situation.

Despite having just started a new job, Bonnie attended

the trial every day. She knew it put her employment in jeopardy, but she had to be there for her ex-husband, Ejaz.

It seemed to be the beginning of a long time of misfortune for Bonnie. Bonnie was suffering severe depression, and was having extreme difficulty eating or sleeping, resulting in feeling constantly  exhausted, both emotionally and physically. She was having problems remembering things. "I am hurting so badly; the pain is unbearable," she told family members. Sometimes she lashed out. "I know Leah had it all planned! She thought it all out before she did it! Before she was ever strung out on drugs!" Ejaz had already helped so many people; Bonnie conceded that perhaps "his mission in life was over." In between the angry outbursts and crying jags, she began to drink heavily.

Her family members knew exactly how she felt. Others told them it would get better, while some advised them to "just move on." *Move on?* Ernestine Marsh was appalled. Having lost two husbands, two children, and having escaped one abusive marriage, she knew that, no matter how emotionally strong a person is, there is no just "getting over it."

Ejaz's ex-sister in law Johnny Joy handled her grief by researching the case. She threw herself into work, looking up records and jotting down notes. She studied legal issues and case precedents. She kept the family updated on how the legal system operated. She did not attend the trial. It was more than she could handle.

Those scheduled to testify had to wait outside the courtroom before they were allowed into the courtroom to take the stand. Ernestine and her family shifted on the cushioned benches in the hallway, leaning back against the wall, checking their watches while looking at the closed court room doors, wondering what was taking place on the other side.

They were not the only people in the hallway who were ruminating over the case. Leah's family was there as well. It was so difficult. How does the family of the murdered begin communication with the family of the murderer?

After a recess, Jordan, now fourteen, was finally called to the stand to testify. He noted, that during the break, Leah had changed clothes. *They're trying to fool me*, he thought as he settled into the witness stand. *They're trying to mess with me, thinking I won't know who she is because now she looks different.*

"Can you point out that person today, in the courtroom?" he was being asked.

Without blinking, he raised his slender arm and pointed at Leah. "She's right there," he said clearly.

He was a mature fourteen, but he sometimes felt confused by the questions the defense attorney asked him. It was not easy to sit in front of a room packed with people to talk about such private matters. *Strange*, he thought. *I don't feel anything for Leah. I thought I would be mad, or sad. I don't even hate her. Mostly I'm just disappointed. She looks sincerely upset. She knows she hurt a lot of people.*

Once he had testified, Jordan was able to sit in the gallery with his relatives who had testified before him. During the trial, crime scene pictures were shown on a big screen for all those in the courtroom to see. No one had told Jordan he was going to see pictures of his father's decomposing, mutilated body enlarged ten times larger than life-size. Jordan was still in shock, and in addition to losing his mentor and hero, he now had to grapple with images of Ejaz's remains. He knew now exactly what had happened. And Leah, someone he had truly liked and trusted, was to blame.

Leah's change of clothing was not the only problem in identifying the defendant. One of her attorneys had placed his chair so that he blocked Leah from the view of anyone on the witness stand. During the trial, one witness for the prosecution asked if they might step down from the stand to identify Leah, which was granted. After walking slowly across the room and passing the Judge's bench, the witness pointed out the wrong person as Leah Joy Ward. Leah's mother, on the stand, could not identify her daughter until the attorney shifted and kicked his chair back. She then saw Leah, who sat demurely behind the desk, and identified her for the court.

The state had to carefully select what crime scene photos they would show to the court. They needed to show the body, walk the jury through the incident, but they did not want to use shock value to influence or distance the jurors.

Still, when the graphic photos were shown to the jury, one juror's stomach began to rumble and she began to heave. The courtroom froze when the juror vomited into her hands. Nonetheless, the juror, despite having a queasy stomach, assured the court that she felt she could continue to listen to testimony and make a fair and unbiased decision.

Bonnie Garrett had a lot of time to examine her feelings when sitting outside and, finally, inside the courtroom. As the trial wore on, she remained silent. She just was simply not able to discuss the loss, her feelings, or anything remotely connected to the crime. She was disgusted with Leah, who sat there modestly dressed like a housewife who was about to go shopping. Still, she could not feel any ill will towards the woman. Bonnie hoped Leah's family was able to visit Leah when she was behind bars. Bonnie felt sympathy for Leah's family, who did seem sincerely wounded by their child's life. *She could have been so much more,* Bonnie thought, looking at the woman with the carefully curled hair and full makeup. *Instead, she chose this path. I don't want her to suffer, but she has to pay for what she did.*

Larry Ward was coming off the tugboat, having returned to work on the river he loved, when he heard the news. He called Leah's mother and asked her what happened, was it *the* Leah Ward who was being tried for murder?

Yes, Leah's mother sobbed. Leah would not talk to her own mother, but she was in serious trouble. Leah had called her the day before her interrogation, saying Ejaz was dead and she was a suspect. Now they all knew that Leah had probably killed Ejaz Ahmad.

Larry refused to believe it, so he went to the courthouse, slipping in quietly to observe the trial. He instantly recognized his wife, though he had not seen her for some time. There she sat, her hair cut in a short, curly red cap around her face. She was dressed modestly and, to Larry, appeared to be in shock.

The prosecution saw Leah's sedate behavior as an act. "She's trying to look like a good girl," Pamela Fleming thought. "Like the poor, defenseless victim of abuse. Which, I know, she is *not*." The work now was to prove it to a jury.

The trial date was November 1, 2005. Would a jury believe the prosecution, or the defense?

# CHAPTER 46

The courtroom was silent as the audio recording of the 9-1-1 call from May 1, 2003, echoed throughout the courtroom.

The caller told the operator she was "calling for this la... I'm calling 9-1-1...uh, this lady came over here looking for her hus ... father-in-law. She found a dead body in – in the ... in this house."

The caller handed Ernestine the telephone, and Ernestine's frantic voice now filled the courtroom. She could not remember the Sea Isle address. She told the operator, "it's – it's my grandson. We come over here to see about his daddy because ..." She admitted she was so nervous that she could not think clearly.

"Don't start crying," the operator told her.

Ernestine managed to explain about retrieving the chicken and the stench in the shed. She shakily explained how Ejaz had gone missing.

"You want me to start an ambulance?"

"No, I don't know. This ... this body's dead. It's got flies uh, all around it and it's covered up with a piece of plastic ... and I don't know."

The operator clarified it was the son-in-law that was in the shed and the grandson who was standing with Ernestine. "Is he okay?" she asked of the grandson.

"No, I'm the one who's not okay," Ernestine answered the even toned voice on the end of the line. "I mean he's standing here by me. No, he's not okay, not my little grandson, he's not okay either. This is a bad thing!" She began to explain about Leah, and her moving out, and about the various excuses Leah gave them of Ejaz's whereabouts. "She told lies."

The operator assured Ernestine, "We're gonna get someone out, okay?"

"All right honey." She thanked the operator, and told her, "I want to call my daughter."[9]

When the call ended, silence engulfed the room, with the exception of a few people clearing their throats or shifting in their seats.

Leah did not take the stand, so her statement made to the Memphis police on May 5 had to be admitted. Pamela Fleming introduced the statement and called Detective Webb to the stand, one of the two officers who had interviewed Leah on May 5, 2003.

Fleming read Leah's statement to the court, and then proceeded to read from the transcript with Webb, with her reading the questions the officers had asked, and Webb responding with Leah's answers, both reading from their separate copies of the transcript. They were both careful to read in even tones, without displays of emotions, but what they read caused chills in many observers.

Q: After you shot Ejaz, what did you do?

A: After I walked around the block I stayed for days. I don't know how many. I just sat down beside him…it had been weeks, and the smell was strong, and I opened the bathroom door and saw worms coming out of his head – coming out of him. Okay. I tried to clean up the worms, and shut the door … One day I came in there and tried to get his body out but I couldn't. I cleaned up around the area where the blood and the worms – I didn't know where it was. His head is like – just hold on – his head is like corroded, so I panicked, and I cut his head off because the worms was coming out of his mouth and I was scared.

Q: What did you do with Ejaz's body?

A: At first I dragged it out in the front yard. It was around twelve something at night. I got scared, so I dragged him in the back yard and put him in the shop in the back.

Q: How long did (the body) stay in the shed?

---

9    Excerpt from "911 Tape from May 01, 2003 at 17:35:24, victim Ejaz Ahmad, defendant-Leah Ward, AG File AJ4903, indict #03-04434"

A: At least two or three days, because I had to surrender on Wednesday.

One of Leah's attorneys, Mr. Sayle, cross-examined the detective. He explained that the confession was not recorded, that it was Leah's initials handwritten by Leah on the confession. Detective Webb testified how she had observed one bruise when Leah showed it to her, but it had not been photographed nor notated. Webb could not say exactly where the bruise was located due to the passage of time between the interview and the trial.

One person involved in the case who sought justice for Ejaz was not able to testify or see the investigation through. During his testimony, Detective Webb explained that Sergeant Sims, who had conducted the interview with Webb, was now deceased due to a boating accident. The department lost an excellent investigator and a fine officer the day they buried Sergeant Larry Sims.

As Ernestine sat in the gallery with her family she stared at Leah with a turmoil mixture of emotions that left her nauseous. "Ejaz did everything he could to help her," she ruminated, "and she killed him. She killed him!" Watching Leah, the thought ran through Ernestine's mind that Leah was the same age as her granddaughter.

Leah's devastated family also sat in the gallery to hear closing arguments.

Missy Branham had worked carefully on closing arguments, describing how Leah had cut through thigh and neck bones. "That's not someone who's afraid. All of these actions were done to make it look like nothing happened. What she did to that man was criminal."

"She had the ability to leave," Prosecutor Pam Fleming told the jury in her closing arguments. "The first thing she did was get rid of the gun. You have to decide if this is a cold-blooded, heartless killer."

The defense continued with their argument that Leah killed in self-defense. "Then she panicked," Kathy Kent told the jury. "She was scared. You have to consider her mental state at the time of the killing."

On November 4, 2005, both the defense and prosecution rested. Judge Beasley orally briefed and provided each member of the jury with a thick packet of instructions to be followed in order to decide the defendant's guilt or innocence. After listening attentively, they were dismissed to make the decision as to the fate of Leah Joy Ward.

Deliberations are perhaps the most nerve-wracking part of a trial. Will the jury take hours or days? What is the conversation behind those doors? This jury was being asked to decide the fate of a woman who sat only so many feet away, whose face they had seen.

Just over two hours later, the jury sent a note that they had reached a verdict.

# CHAPTER 47

It is always a tense moment when the members of a jury file back into the courtroom and take their seats after deliberation. Both the defense and the prosecution ruminate over the fine points of the presentation of their cases. Those in the gallery are forced to remain silent when all they want to do is release a flood of emotions which they've suppressed throughout the trial. The defendant's emotions run the gamut. It is as if the entire courtroom holds its breath until the verdict is announced.

"Guilty of first degree murder" rang out through the silence.

Larry, not watching the jury, was instead focused on Leah's face. She did not move, but her eyes widened as big as silver dollars. "She actually thought she was going to get out of this one," he muttered. "She really thought she was going to walk out of here scot free."

Leah was sentenced to life in prison. Barring a miracle, she would spend the next fifty one years behind bars.

Pamela and Missy let out sighs of relief, knowing their job was well done. It would not bring Ejaz back, or undo the trail of damage Leah had left, but it was justice. Pamela later said, "It was all just very, very sad. Ejaz seemed to be an awesome guy."

When the officers prepared the restraints to handcuff Leah and take her away to a holding cell, she twisted around in her seat. Her blue eyes, filled with tears, met Jordan's brown ones. "I'm sorry," she whispered softly to him. "I'm so sorry."

Leah's photo, along with the words "Life Sentence" in big, bold letters, made the cover of a Memphis newspaper. The case had been titillating, a woman accused of decapitation and sexual mutilation made for interesting copy.

MacArthur Borner was serving time for his role in the

Selmer, Tennessee, drug bust when a friend told him some startling news.

"Did you hear about Leah?" the friend asked. MacArthur had had no contact with Leah since their sentencing for the drug conviction. "What about her?"

"She chopped some dude's head off," the friend reported, "and she's in prison."

Initially, MacArthur could not believe it. Leah, committing murder? He knew she could be a sweet girl, but he had seen her do some mean things, and she was an uncontrollable viper when angered. "I have my daddy's temper," she had once told him. He remembered her laughing, trying to learn to play chess, smiling that bright, gap-toothed smile. Still … a murderer?

Had to be the drugs, MacArthur Bonner told himself. Crack was an evil drug, easy to get hooked, sure to fry your brain.

# CHAPTER 48

Ernestine Marsh and Bonnie went to the storage shed at Storage USA, where Leah had stored all of Ejaz's things. It took weeks to go through it all, for Leah had just crammed and shoved everything into the storage area. Ernestine found crumbled pictures that Leah's children had drawn "to mom." There were more photographs of Leah's kids, Ejaz, and Jordan. There was a black negligee. Bonnie found crumpled pages, the marriage and the divorce records for Bonnie and Ejaz. She did find Ejaz's bedroom suite, which she gave to Jordan.

They picked through the items, stepping carefully over and around the miscellaneous furniture pieces. One of the items was Leah's satchel, the satchel she used for packing her scrubs and a few necessities when she went to work at the hospital. Ernestine opened the satchel and found Leah's neatly folded scrubs. Under the scrubs, she found a pair of stiletto high heels, lace panties, and a few daring items of lingerie. Ernestine dug deeper into the bag, and what she found next made her sink down into a chair. They were nude photos of Leah, posing provocatively for the camera. Ernestine knew these pictures were not taken for Ejaz.

Bonnie started a small bonfire in the side yard of her home, watching the red and yellow flames slowly catch, feeding into the other. When she was satisfied with the size of the fire, she reached into a bag and withdrew one of Leah's negligees and dropped it into the fire. Bonnie watched as the sheer cloth melted and disappeared.

She withdrew another item of clothing, dropping it into the fire.

One by one, she dropped the items she had gathered belonging to Leah Joy Ward and let the fire engulf them, the reflection of the flames in her tear-filled eyes. She took a stick and rousted the embers, ensuring it was all gone.

Everything she had that was Leah's, or reminded her of Leah, was reduced to ashes and dust.

Bonnie stared into the fire for a while, until she felt somewhat vindicated. "Burn in hell," she whispered to Leah; "Ejaz is somewhere in heaven."

# CHAPTER 49

Leah's attorneys insisted she refrain from writing letters to Judge Beasley. "But Judge Beasley, this is not fair" she wrote to him on November 16, 2005. She insisted she had fought for her life the day she shot Ejaz. Yes, she admitted to killing him, but it was not premeditated. "I am not lieing [*Sic*]," she wrote, "I am willing to take all and any kind of tests to prove ... I did not plot the murder..." "I am not trying to justify my behavior because a lot of things I do not remember," she explained.

On November 28, 2005, friends of Ejaz collectively wrote a letter to District Attorney Bill Gibbons, demanding to know why Leah did not receive the death penalty, speculating that it may have been a case of discrimination against Muslims, inferring that if Ejaz were not Muslim, Leah's sentence would have been harsher. They carefully researched past cases and D.A. Gibbon's record in court. The group wondered why, whenever they attempted to get answers about the case, they were ignored or shunned. "All we seek," they wrote, "is fair justice for Ejaz." Copies were sent to prosecutors Missy Branham, Pam Fleming, and Judge Beasley.

Leah received "time served" for her time spent sitting in the Shelby County Jail from September 3, 2003, to February 5, 2005, which meant those days would be credited to her prison time. This meant little, for she was going to be in custody for the rest of her life, barring a miracle.

In 2005, she was transferred to the Tennessee Prison for Women (TPW) on December 15, just one day before her 29th birthday. Ruminating over such a sorry birthday, she sat in the back of the transport vehicle, watching Shelby County disappear behind her as Nashville, Tennessee, loomed ahead. She had four hours to contemplate her fate as she was driven to Tennessee's primary correctional facility for females.

During the initial classification summary, she was asked

for her religious preference; Leah told the intake officer she was "Christian." She told them she had thirteen years of formal education. Her weight was up to 167 pounds, thanks to the starch-filled jailhouse food. She explained the list of psychotropic drugs she had been prescribed, explaining she had been taking her medication up to the day she was transported to prison. As she stood there answering questions, she surely must have contemplated the fact that she was not yet thirty years old, and she was going to grow old behind bars?

She told the intake officer that her first husband's physical abuse landed her a trip to the hospital, where she was treated for black eyes, bruises, and a broken nose. She said her second husband was just as abusive, his hitting her had caused bruises and head injuries. Each husband had raped her one time each, she said, forcing sex on her. It was also noted how she was raped, per her self-report, by two or three men in the MMHI.

While her scores on the Sexual Victim and Predator Predictor showed there were no current indications that she was a sexual victim, recommendations were made for her to participate in the 12-Step program, the domestic violence group, grief counseling, a group for women who suffered sexual abuse, and a program called "Thinking for a Change." It was also recommended that she not be placed in general population due to mental health issues. The team would reevaluate that decision in six weeks.

Leah was issued prison clothing and basic toiletries, and then led into the maximum-security prison where up to 760 other female inmates languished, from death row to the lower security inmates. Women worked, ate, slept, and lived out their sentences inside that tall fence. Some of them were on work release, meaning they left the institution to go work in the "free world" and then returned by curfew. Some were pre-release, anxiously counting the months, then the days, and, finally, the hours before they left – for good this time -

they swore.

During inmate orientation, Leah listened as she was told of the prison's child visitation program for incarcerated mothers. It had received national recognition, and became a blueprint for other programs. A TPW Warden, Penny Bernhardt, understood the system might be able to cull recidivism if female inmates were able to bond with their young children, thus a weekend visitation program was put in place: children from three months up to their sixth birthday enter the facility at 5:00 pm on a Friday for their designated weekend with mommy. The inmates stay in quarters away from their housing unit, several beds to a room with a crib as needed, spending time with the children. Warden Bernhardt was instrumental in not only developing the program, but also in ensuring it remained a continued success. Warden Bernhardt arranged for the women and children in the program to have a place to enjoy meals in a family environment, indoor and outdoor recreation, and the mothers were taught ways to help their child's social development, albeit prison rules and regulations remained in place. On Sunday afternoon, the children wave goodbye from the arms of their caregivers, leaving a mom smiling through their tears as they blow kisses goodbye. Participating mothers cannot be classified as greater than Medium Security Level, nor have a disciplinary infraction on their records for a given time period; the disciplinary levels and dates varied. For example, if the inmate had a Class "A" charge (the most serious of infractions), they had to wait nine months before being allowed to participate. Besides nurturing the mother-child bond, the program also rewarded good behavior while it worked to also minimize serious infraction incidents, and helped the women create goals, something sorely lacking in most of them.

Leah learned of the academic programs offered at TPW, such as obtaining a GED, or enrolling in programs such as cosmetology, culinary arts, or classes to learn computers skills. They were offered the potential to learn necessary skills which would enable them to gain a job, upon release, that paid enough to support a single mother and her two children, the average for women in prison.

During her time in TPW, Leah was informed that she could participate in therapeutic treatment programs. The Correctional Recovery Academy was a 64-bed program that focused on drug and alcohol treatment. "Fast Track" was a life skills and job readiness program for up to forty women at a time who were transitioning from release into the "free world."

The programs are there for inmates who want to take advantage of them. All of the programs, from the cost of obtaining a GED to therapy, are free of cost to inmates, courtesy of Tennessee taxpayers, who are saddled with the daily cost of, on average, about $75 per day for each inmate.

During the inmate orientation, it was strongly recommended that inmates stay out of trouble because breaking the rules could mean everything from a verbal warning to a change in security classification. The latter meant loss of many privileges and a move to a different building. Class "A" infractions were the most serious. Class "C" infractions were less serious. A "verbal warning" could be given for less serious infractions, which meant no formal write up, but it would be noted on the inmate's disciplinary record. In prison, when one enjoys few freedoms, losing just one privilege can be devastating.

"Inmates have twenty-four hours a day, seven days a week to think about two things: getting out, and getting over," said one correctional officer who spent a career working both male and female institutions, from minimum to maximum security levels. "They will spend a lot of time, energy, and money (either their own or the taxpayer's) vying to be released even one day earlier; they will spend time trying to figure out how to 'get over' the rules, regulations, officers, the system." Inmates know which officer is a pushover, which officer is a stickler for rules, which staff member can be "played" and even possibly "turned" into performing illegal acts such as smuggling in contraband, allowing the inmate to break rules without punishment, or becoming sexually involved with those incarcerated.

Leah worked in "Foundations Culinary Arts I," meaning the prison kitchen, at the pay of seventeen cents an hour from January to May 2006. That January, she reported to the doctors that she suffered panic attacks when she was in a small space, and that she was afraid to go outside, classic symptoms of agoraphobia. In July, she reported the panic attacks and anxiety fluctuated, and her appetite and ability to sleep were altered. Her thoughts were racing madly through her head, and her energy and hyperactivity were so enhanced that she could not do anything for long without losing concentration. She reported the symptoms were the same in January of 2007. Her self-esteem was suffering as a result.

Leah received a job change in May 2007, working Core Carpentry at thirty-four cents an hour. She was also diagnosed with an anxiety disorder.

Leah was already street-wise, and had done time in prison, so she fit into the culture immediately. She knew which inmates had her back, what few officers might succumb to an offer of sex or a bribe, how to play the game and stay out of trouble or, at least, not get caught. Many officers and staff had settled into a predictable way of doing things. There was enough time to study those patterns and use that information to an advantage.

But she slipped up and was charged with larceny in March 2008. She pleaded innocent but was found guilty a few days later. About six months later, she was caught with drugs, and again, she pleaded innocent but was found guilty after the investigation.

On April 23, 2008, Leah was transferred from TPW to the Mark Luttrell Correction Center for a classification reassignment.

Her record shows she worked in the kitchen from April 28 to July 2008, her pay starting at thirty-four cents an hour and ending at forty-two cents per hour.

Meanwhile, she continued filing motions. She had secured a job in the prison law library as an aid, now making fifty cents an hour. Leah read law books voraciously, meticulously copying down information into a tablet. Her letter writing also remained a constant, including one in which she made a request for information on her case to Memphis Mayor A.C. Wharton, which generated a reply from the Criminal Court Clerk's Offices.

In January of 2010, a psychiatrist saw Leah. She now reported being sexually abused as a child, alleging that she had been molested between the ages of five to ten. "I blocked it out a lot," she further claimed. She maintained that her father and both of her husbands had been physically abusive, which culminated in the murder of her second husband. "He was trying to kill me. I took his life only so I could get away." She had dropped out of school but did have her GED and some college. "I've been angry," she reported, as to why she cut her hair. She said she had tried to commit suicide twice, once by attempting to overdose, and the other time she had cut herself. She was recently in a relationship, but because it triggered memories of the abuse, she was forced to end it.

A mental health treatment plan was completed for Leah. The plan included monitoring her for mania, nightmares, auditory hallucinations, and anxiety. She was also placed on medication, which would be monitored carefully. Some patients react well to certain medications, yet cannot cope with another. All of the medication has side effects, and no two medications have the same exact effect on different people. It can be a balancing act to find the right medication and dosage for a right person.

Another April report revealed that Leah had begun to attend a group where they focused on deep breathing, relaxation, and visualization for stress management. She reported that the slow, rhythmic breathing exercises seemed to help her, as she could feel some of the stress ebbing out of her body.

She returned to her job in the law library, delving into the thick books. With her pencil scratching across paper, she formulated her plans to beat the legal system.

As on the streets, Leah could not seem to stay out of trouble, and in May of 2011, she was caught and written up for her behavior when someone pissed her off and she stood up to them, causing her to receive an infraction for fighting. This time she owned up to it, confessing her role in the fight. Things heated up about a month later when she was charged with both assault and assault on staff, both deemed as class "A" infractions. She pleaded guilty two days later and received her punishment. She managed to stay out of trouble, or, at least, did not get caught for the rest of that year.

Her psychiatric treatment plan ended in May 2011. She had reported the nightmares, paranoia, and anxiety had dropped down, and she was no longer hearing voices. She lost the beloved law library position and returned to work in the kitchen, her salary dipping to thirty-four cents an hour. The next month, she returned to TPW. She began working with computers from August to September of 2011.

Seven years to the date of when she first arrived at TPW, Leah was caught with a deadly weapon. She pled innocent but was found guilty of this Class "A" infraction.

Still, Leah continued to file motions from prison. She wrote Kevin Key, the Criminal Court Clerk, in March 2012 requesting legal records. She had become adept at filing motions. She sent a packet of information along with her motion for a retrial. She handwrote the tabs and included copies of her job applications and mental health records. Under a cover page labeled "New Evidence(s)" she included copies of pages from an unknown source about PTSD, Battered Women's Syndrome, and legal issues involving each.

Each time she sent any document, from appendixes to affidavits verifying medical history, psychiatric evaluations, and legal forms, the information became public record.

She held various jobs, including working in the kitchen, planting flowers, maintaining the lawns, and as a painter, from 2013 through 2015. For a short stint in March, she was paid thirty-four cents hourly for assisting the mental health department.

Leah's record of behavior was never spotless. After all, this was her new home, and she had never followed the rules anywhere she lived. In 2013, she was given a verbal warning because she had interfered with an officer's duties, and rang in the new year of 2014 by refusing a staff member's direct order which resulted in her receiving another verbal warning. Towards the end of the year, she was caught out of boundaries, fighting yet again. Both were classified as "C" infractions. She pleaded guilty. Leah still wielded her charming personality; she also continued to harbor that infamous temper.

While incarcerated in TPW, Leah learned how the other inmates used the cyber world to meet people on "the outside." They put ads on the websites of organizations that paired inmates with pen pals. The women wrote profiles describing how they sought friendship, love, someone to be with when released, or just someone to exchange letters with in order to alleviate the sheer boredom of being incarcerated. Soon Leah followed suit, carefully writing her own ad. Then she dressed neatly, carefully applied her makeup and red lipstick, and styled her hair into a short coif with a pink bow atop her head. She paid out of her commissary to have a picture taken on "Picture Day" and sent it to an online inmate pen-pal service, along with her description of herself.

She wrote that she was looking for lasting, good friendship, people who also enjoyed writing letters. Leah was very good at writing, she promised. She was good with languages, wanting to learn both Spanish and Hebrew. Law remained a great interest. She ensured she looked good by working out and dancing to music, a passion of hers. She tried to stay busy, always working on education, creative outlets, expressing herself.

Besides being creative and intelligent, Leah assured her potential friends that she was pretty – and just as beautiful in her soul and mind.

She later altered her information. She asked for encouraging, positive friends who could help her become an even better person, friends who she could also encourage as she was a down to earth, fun loving country girl at heart. She explained she was once a nurse, and she dreamed of becoming a paralegal or returning to college. She is still working on her Spanish. She was busy in prison, with church, reading and television, dancing and exercising in between work.

Leah also listed herself on a website created by the New York based Lighthouse International, a religious-based organization whose mission statement was "to lead people worldwide into a growing relationship with Jesus Christ by putting God's love into action." It boasts a publishing company, outreach for youth, veterans, Native Americans, the homeless, and incarcerated persons. There are two "outreach" programs in Pakistan. On this website, Leah is listed as Leah Joy Ward – Ahmad.

Maybe, Leah hoped, she would meet someone really special, a nice man who cared about her, who would take care of her. Nothing was impossible.

# CHAPTER 50

The investigation was over, the trial was old news in the media, and Ejaz's friends and family went about trying to pick up the pieces of their lives. Like all other family members of victims of such violent crimes, they learned life was now split in two parts: Before Ejaz was killed, and after his death.

Ejaz had been sending money to family in Pakistan. His sister was handicapped as a result of a fall; he always ensured she had crutches and money for medical bills. He had been sending money to his sister's two daughters so they could afford college. If someone in his family needed medical care, Ejaz sent them money. Now that he was gone, there was no one else to help his family.

Though mature for his age, Jordan was still a boy, and he felt angry that his father was gone. He could feel it rise up in his throat at times, trying to choke him.

Jordan confided in Ernestine about his dreams, just as his father also had confided in her not too long ago. He was growing tall and slender, with dark hair and eyes, so much like Ejaz. His family wanted him to remain close to be able to listen to him and comfort him. Jordan was a very special young man, and the last blood connection they had to their beloved Ejaz Ahmad.

The family still had unanswered questions. No one had been allowed to speak to Leah during the investigation or the trial, and now she would have to place them on her visitation list to visit her in prison. They wanted to know why she didn't just leave town instead of killing him? Why did she have to desecrate the body? So many whys.

# CHAPTER 51

Jordan, Johnny Joy, Ernestine, and Bonnie visited with a friend in Ernestine's cozy living room, where they shared pictures and memories of Ejaz, and laughed about the fun and kindness he brought into their lives. Their soft, southern voices dipped and rose caused by the fluctuation of emotions the memories evoked.

"He was a handsome man," Johnny Joy said, pointing out his dimples, in a close-up photo of a smiling, successful Ejaz.

Another photograph, a professionally done portrait of Ejaz holding baby Jordan, now sits in a prominent place in the room, poised as if its subjects were listening in on their conversation.

Jordan considered aloud a question. If he could talk to Leah, what would he say? "It took me a while, but I have to forgive her," he said. "If I didn't forgive her, it would eat me alive. I'll never forget my dad." He thought for a moment. "You know … one day, I may reach out to Leah, eventually. Maybe I can help her. I'd ask her, what was going on in her head? It's sad, you know? The whole thing's sad. I've lost a parent, but so have her kids. I feel sorry for her kids." He has not attempted to contact Christopher or Sallie. "But they can call me anytime, in case they want to ask me some questions."

Ernestine knows what she would say if she could talk to Leah. "If I could say anything to Leah, I'd ask her, why did she do it? Did she act alone? I didn't ever get a chance to confront her. Ejaz was the best man I've ever known," she says emphatically. "He was a wonderful father, a good son, and I loved him. I still love him."

Johnny Joy wonders if she could write Leah, but then decides she doesn't "want to give her the satisfaction of receiving a letter."

Bonnie said she still has the jewelry and clothing Ejaz had made for her. "I have some amazing things he gave me," she said tearfully, "besides love." Of Leah Ward, she asserts, "I am very disappointed when I think about (the crime), even now; I was never spiteful, not even today. I don't wish ill will towards her because she has a family. I hope her family can visit her. Mostly I am just disgusted with her. He was the last person who should've been taken away." Bonnie thought about Ejaz for a moment. "He was a versatile, multi-talented multifaceted man. He gave my family amazing memories by doing his part to make the world a better place." She stopped to wipe away tears. "If there were more like him, the world would be more peaceful." It took her a moment to compose herself, before adding, "Leah took him away, but she did not take away his love, or the memories his family has of him. Ejaz is in our hearts all of the time."

# CHAPTER 52

*No man dies before his time.*
*-Last Will & Testament of Ejaz Ahmad*

Ejaz had written a last will and testament. After the costs of his legal debts and burial expenses, Ejaz had divided his assets as follows: a percentage was to be divided equally among four religious-based organizations. Under Article V, Schedule A, there existed a standard clause that read:

*Should I die as a result of murder, I direct that the adjured murderer ... shall be disqualified to receive any part of my estate.*

The remainder of his assets was divided as follow: Jordan was to receive the largest percentage, and two nieces back home in Pakistan were to receive a small each, and Ejaz specifically requested that these funds be used for their education. He entrusted Bonnie to ensure that Jordan would continue with his Islamic education.

Perhaps the most poignant of his will was on page one, under the Preamble, which read in part:

*I remind (friends and family) that no man dies before his time. The exact duration of each life span is determined before we are born ... Death is tragic only for the one who lived out his life in self-deception ... do not preoccupy yourselves with my death, but instead make the proper preparations for your own.*

It was poignant, sweet, and sad ... as is life.

# AFTERWORD

On September 11, 2001, the world watched as the Twin Towers in New York City crumpled to the earth, carrying thousands to their death. Subsequent attacks followed. The perpetrators were Muslim extremists. Many Americans became suspicious, even violent, towards people of the Muslim faith. It appeared that many seemed to believe that if someone came from the Middle East, he or she was dangerous, someone to be mistrusted and feared, perhaps even a terrorist.

Like the Bible and other religious texts, the Qur'an also contains passages of violence. There are Muslims who lead a life devoted to nonviolence, just as there are Jews, Christians, and Buddhists devoted to peace. There are Muslims who commit crimes, just as there are also Jews, Christians, and Buddhists guilty of committing domestic violence, theft, murder, and more.

According to a 2010 study, it is estimated that there are 1.6 billion adherents to the Islamic religion worldwide. It is the second largest religious tradition after Christianity, with reportedly 2.2 billion adherents. Muslims make up a little more than twenty-three percent of the world's religions.

The Muslim religion is not the only religion that appears to place women in subservient roles. The Church of Christ does not allow women to be church elders. Women cannot be Catholic priests. Historically, Jewish women were discouraged from learning Talmud. In reality, there are far less female religious leaders in all religions than there are male leaders.

Religious beliefs and interpretations have always been a part of world culture and history. Many wars have been fought over religious ideology.

There are radical extremists in each religion. To compare all Muslims to Mohamed Atta (an Egyptian who was one of the ring leaders responsible for 9/11) is akin to comparing all Baptists to the Westboro Baptist Church (a Kansas-based church certified as a hate group).

Because of the public feelings and political backlash of terrorism by extremists who are Muslim, or who appear Middle Eastern, Ernestine Marsh worries for the safety of Jordan and Drake. Both are swarthy, obviously Middle Eastern. "They could be in danger just because of the way they look," Ernestine explains. She shook her head, saying, "I worry what someone, who doesn't know any better, could do to them."

Ernestine Marsh still lives near Memphis, Tennessee. She experienced another tragedy when her home burned and she was forced to rebuild. Although it set her back in some ways, it did not destroy her positive outlook on life. She still loves to dress stylishly and usually includes a hat in her ensemble.

Ejaz's only son lives with Ernestine. Handsome and articulate, Jordan shares a knack for electronics and is multitalented like his father, and has chosen to study computer science at college. "My father was a kind person who loved his family, loved his son, and wanted the best for all of us. He was kind, and he cared about everybody. He didn't deserve what happened to him."

Bonnie found nothing made her feel better, so she began heavily drinking, until she began making active decisions on healthy ways to overcome her grief. She began by going to a gym, which impacted her food choices as well, and soon she starting singing and studying music again. "I'm also working on my mind," she reported. "I am getting better. I can think more clearly and make better decisions." The panic attacks and nightmares are now rare, but she does not venture far from home. She rarely trusts anyone, and going outside her comfort zone of work, the gym, and home causes her anxiety. "I'm working on that," she says, years after the trial resulting in Leah's conviction. Despite being married to Raymond for over twenty years, she still has issues with her husband because of Ejaz. "I will always love him, and I love him still," she unapologetically tells Raymond. "But I also love you." To another friend she explained, "I miss Ejaz's presence and his warmth, but I always feel his love." Bonnie wiped away tears. "He is in my heart," she vowed, "all of the time."

Bonnie's sister Johnny Joy confirmed, when speaking of Ejaz, "We all liked him. And I still have some things he gave me from Pakistan. Ejaz was a giver; he loved giving presents." She was hit with another tragedy later in life with the death of her own son. Today, she is an animal rights advocate, throwing herself into personally investigating and fighting against puppy mills and inhumane treatment of dogs. Her philanthropy keeps her sane, and she works tirelessly.

Memphis Police Department Lieutenant Walter Norris is now retired after serving for thirty-one years in the police department and city he loves. He continues to reside in Memphis, where he writes fictional murder mysteries. Norris' first book, "Adventitious," has received excellent reviews. His oldest daughter is a police officer, carrying on the family tradition.

Johnny Smith, Jr., resides in a small town near Memphis. He continues to have strange dreams of his best friend, Ejaz, and misses him every day.

Leah's family continues on without her, anguished that all of their efforts to help her, and prayers on her behalf, have seemed to be for naught.

From time to time, Leah's children visit their mother where she is incarcerated. When they were young, their maternal grandmother took them to visit their mother in 2006 shortly after Leah was incarcerated at TPW. The kids sat silently while their grandmother and mom chatted. Leah tried to engage them, but received only disinterested responses, as they did not know her.

Larry Ward still lives in the town where he was born

and raised. He misses working on the boat, but he is kept busy with Christopher and Sallie and being a grandfather to Sallie's baby. He is still energetic, with a dry sense of humor. He tries to date but claims, "all I meet are crazy women." Larry knows marriage is probably not in his future: He has yet to legally divorce Leah. She writes him and the kids on occasion, sending pictures taken of herself by the prison photographer during "Photo Days." Larry says the correspondence quickly finds its way into the trash. Leah recently wrote him, asking for forgiveness. "What am I supposed to forgive?" He shakes his head. "I'm not God."

Ejaz was laid to rest in a cemetery in Mumford, Tennessee, where Muslim brothers and sisters are also buried. A friend paid for the services and the burial expenses. One family member says she still feels his spirit, and it is restless.

Missy Branham has retired after a successful career of working for the Shelby County District Attorney's offices.

Pamela Fleming is now the Assistant District Attorney for Shelby County in Memphis. She recently married an investigator in the Cold Case Division. Both recall the Ward Case and Leah's behavior. Pamela still practices an unwritten rule homicide detectives taught her, to never say, "I've seen it all" because the next case might be even more heinous or sadistic. Two of her subsequent cases as a prosecutor proved the mantra to be good practice:

In 2008, Jessie Dotson, thirty-three, of Memphis, shot and killed his brother Cecil, Cecil's girlfriend, their children, and a family friend. Jessie killed them with a semi-automatic handgun, then bludgeoned and stabbed them. The children ranged in ages from nine years to two months old. The baby miraculously survived a knife wound through its skull. Even for veteran investigators, the crime scene was gruesome.

Another case file was dropped on Pamela Fleming's desk involving a Shelby County husband and father who murdered his wife and raped his fourteen-year-old daughter. Then he took the girl and her younger sibling to shop for a band saw.

Back home, the man forced the girl to hold her dead mother's head while the man used the saw to decapitate the woman. Later, he returned the saw to the store for a refund.

Leah Joy Ward is currently inmate number 00399626 at the Tennessee Prison for Women in Nashville, Tennessee. Pamela Fleming explains: "Prisons retain the ability to reduce sentences for good behavior to help control prison problems. Thus Leah's (life) sentence is fifty-one years. With good behavior credit she would get out in fifty-one years - no parole, just out. Every infraction she has can cost her good credit days. Thus if she is perfectly behaved (in prison) she will get out in 51 years." If she has infractions on her prison record, she will be behind bars for longer than 51 years. Leah's eligibility for release is in 2059 (barring any infractions on her record). She will be 83 years old.

Leah appears on one of TLC's television series, "Prison Diaries" in the episode "A Checkered Past." She accuses Ejaz of forcing her to adapt to Muslim religion: wearing a hijab, going to mosque. She reiterates about her abusive life at the hands of men, including Larry and Ejaz. Again she explains in her careful, slow drawl how Ejaz kicked down the bedroom door to attack her and she was forced to shoot him in self-defense. Lt. Walters, one of Leah's family members, Ernestine Marsh and several family members, and Pamela Fleming appear briefly on the show.

Initially, Leah corresponded with this author. All of her requests, including meeting in person prior to an interview, then to have an attorney present, were agreed upon. When presented with a standard legal document to sign, she destroyed the form and returned it, writing she wished to be left alone and would not endorse the project.[10]

Leah busies herself with filing appeals. She has cited both mental illness and spousal abuse, filing paperwork in an attempt to show Ejaz as abusive and volatile. In one appeal she added copies of her mental health records, legally

10    None of the correspondence appears in this work.

making the information public knowledge.[11]

Only Leah and Ejaz know exactly what happened the day Leah Joy Ward murdered Ejaz Ahmad. Depending on who is to be believed, Leah was either an abused woman defending her life, or a cunning liar who killed Ejaz in cold blood. It is a tragic story of a woman on a road to destruction, and the man who crossed her path. It is a story of conflicting religious values and cultural misunderstandings. The end result is a woman serving life in prison, and a man whose life was tragically cut short.

---

11    Some of the information has been redacted per HIPAA laws, and thus does not appear in this book.

# DOMESTIC ABUSE

*Of men surveyed, 7.4 percent report having been assaulted in their lifetime by a current or former spouse, cohabitating partner, boyfriend, girlfriend, or date.*
*- Full Report of the Prevalence, Incidence, and Consequences of Violence Against Women, U.S. Department of Justice, November 2000, NCJ183781*

Domestic violence is defined as "violent or aggressive behavior within the home, typically involving the violent abuse of a spouse or a partner" by Oxford Dictionary. Domestic Abuse is defined as any incident of threatening behavior, violence or abuse (psychological, physical, sexual, financial or emotional) between adults, who are or have been intimate partners or family members, regardless of gender or sexuality'" In reality, it goes much deeper than mere definition.

The "Power and Control Wheel" displays a visual diagram as a helpful tool to explain the pattern of abusive and violent behaviors used by abusers to establish and maintain control over victims. Like a wheel, it continually spins until someone stops the cycle. "Domestic abuse" is not solely synonymous with physical abuse. It includes using coercion and threats, intimidation, emotional abuse, isolation, children, male privilege, and economic abuse. Minimizing and denying the abuse, and blaming the abuse on the victim, are dynamics which are commonplace for abusers. Statistics and studies have proven emotional violence takes longer to heal than any broken or battered part of the body.

# POWER AND CONTROL WHEEL

Physical and sexual assaults, or threats to commit them, are the most apparent forms of domestic violence and are usually the actions that allow others to become aware of the problem. However, regular use of other abusive behaviors by the batterer, when reinforced by one or more acts of physical violence, make up a larger system of abuse. Although physical assaults may occur only once or occasionally, they instill threat of future violent attacks and allow the abuser to take control of the woman's life and circumstances.

The Power & Control diagram is a particularly helpful tool in understanding the overall pattern of abusive and violent behaviors, which are used by a batterer to establish and maintain control over his partner. Very often, one or more violent incidents are accompanied by an array of these other types of abuse. They are less easily identified, yet firmly establish a pattern of intimidation and control in the relationship.

**VIOLENCE** — physical — sexual

**COERCION AND THREATS:** Making and/or carrying out threats to do something to hurt her. Threatening to leave her, commit suicide, or report her to welfare. Making her drop charges. Making her do illegal things.

**INTIMIDATION:** Making her afraid by using looks, actions, and gestures. Smashing things. Destroying her property. Abusing pets. Displaying weapons.

**MALE PRIVILEGE:** Treating her like a servant: making all the big decisions, acting like the "master of the castle," being the one to define men's and women's roles.

**EMOTIONAL ABUSE:** Putting her down. Making her feel bad about herself. Calling her names. Making her think she's crazy. Playing mind games. Humiliating her. Making her feel guilty.

**ECONOMIC ABUSE:** Preventing her from getting or keeping a job. Making her ask for money. Giving her an allowance. Taking her money. Not letting her know about or have access to family income.

**ISOLATION:** Controlling what she does, who she sees and talks to, what she reads, and where she goes. Limiting her outside involvement. Using jealousy to justify actions.

**USING CHILDREN:** Making her feel guilty about the children. Using the children to relay messages. Using visitation to harass her. Threatening to take the children away.

**MINIMIZING, DENYING, AND BLAMING:** Making light of the abuse and not taking her concerns about it seriously. Saying the abuse didn't happen. Shifting responsibility for abusive behavior. Saying she caused it.

**POWER AND CONTROL**

**VIOLENCE** — physical — sexual

Developed by:
Domestic Abuse Intervention Project
202 East Superior Street
Duluth, MN 55802
218.722.4134

Produced and distributed by:

**NATIONAL CENTER** on Domestic and Sexual Violence
*training · consulting · advisory*
4612 Shoal Creek Blvd. · Austin, Texas 78756
512. 407. 9020 (phone and fax) · www.ncdsv.org

---

The "Cycle of Abuse" is yet another wheel that never stops until someone slams on the brakes to stop the cycle.

1. Tension building - The victim usually lives in a perpetual state of tension. Communications become disjointed, breaking down between the abuser and the abused. The victim's fear rises with the knowledge of what will happen in the future, and in order to slow that process or try to avoid it, the victim will placate the abuser in any way possible, to include involving others (asking the

children to behave a certain way, refusing get-togethers with others for fear it will anger the abuser). Sometimes this phase is referred to as the "walking on eggshells" phase. The victim's job is to keep the abuser calm and happy while tension builds around them, keeping the delicate balance. It is not possible to prevent the second phase in a violent relationship.

2.  Incident - This phase is characterized by incidents of physical, sexual, emotional, religious, and verbal abuse ("You're too stupid to go to school; you're nothing without me") to serious harm (Emergency room visits for physical trauma). At any time the wheel can spin into the next phase.

3.  Reconciliation - The "Reconciliation" or "Honeymoon Phase" is when promises, apologies, and minimizing of the abuser's behavior take place. Some experts on domestic violence prevention education call it the "Time of Roses" because many abusers will bring roses as a gift of apology to the victim. During this phase the abuser becomes the person that the victim loves and wants in their life: attentive, loving, nurturing, a positive influence in everyone's life as loving partner, parent, family member, etc.

4.  Calm Period - The "calm period" is where the abuser may act as if nothing bad has occurred, promises are made, and the victim relies on hope for change. No abuse takes place during this phase. This cycle is where the abuser stops the abuse. Life is filled with hope, happiness, and promises of love and togetherness. It is often referred to as "the honeymoon phase."

The cycle moves forward back to tension building, "walking on eggshells," and back through the entire cycle, over and over again (see illustration).

# Cycle of Abuse

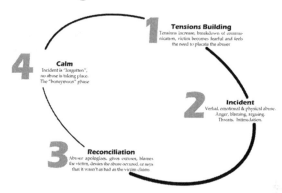

**1 Tensions Building**
Tensions increase, breakdown of communication, victim becomes fearful and feels the need to placate the abuser

**2 Incident**
Verbal, emotional & physical abuse. Anger, blaming, arguing. Threats. Intimidation.

**3 Reconciliation**
Abuser apologizes, gives excuses, blames the victim, denies the abuse occured, or says that it wasn't as bad as the victim claims

**4 Calm**
Incident is "forgotten", no abuse is taking place. The "honeymoon" phase

No one "snaps." People "boil." Akin to a teapot on a hot burner, the waters are cool, then warm, then become boiling, and finally, the whistle blows. The pressure builds up to explosion. The process can only be stopped if the teapot is moved off the burner. As in an abusive relationship, there are warning signs the explosion is coming.

There are often certain indicators that point to the possibility of a potentially violent relationship, which can include:

- One or both partners witnessed abuse as children

- One or both partners abuse alcohol and/or drugs

- Abusers may have a history of cruelty to animals

- A prior history of being abusive and blaming others for one's problems

Often abusers display behaviors such as:

- Quick to form relationships, i.e. claiming to be in love very early in the relationship or wanting to move in together right away

- Has few close personal relationships of their own, and makes active attempts to isolate the victim from his/her support networks

- Constantly checking on the victim, becoming easily jealous
- Often they will blame victims for the abuse
- Often are economically abusive and control the money in the relationship
- Often has an explosive temper, and may strike objects to "blow off steam"
- Painful physical pushing or hitting, calling it "play," or "spanking," etc.
- Name calling and/or using abusive words designed to hurt and then minimizing it by claiming to be playing or kidding
- Uses force or intimidation to dominate or exploit others to get their way in situations
- Having charming, gregarious personalities which can change very quickly to display negative personality traits
- Having the tendency to be easily angered over seemingly insignificant things

Should a friend or family member try to discuss the abuser's behavior with the victim, the abuser will become angry, insisting the friend or family member is jealous, sick, or crazy. He or she may openly side with another abuser in other abusive relationships, stating that the victims "had it coming."

Just as there are characteristics of the perpetrators of abuse, there are common characteristics of abuse victims, to include:

- Poor self esteem, insecure, anxious
- Minimizes or believes abuse is warranted; i.e. self-blaming
- Feels trapped in the situation, doesn't think they can succeed on their own

- May be embarrassed to be in an abusive relationship so won't reach out to others

- May come from a background of abuse

- They tend to have a difficult time with setting boundaries and saying "No"

- They are excessively tolerant and accommodating

- They depend on others, emotionally and financially

- They deceive themselves by thinking that –one day- magically, the abuser will change

- They make excuses for the abuser's behavior and mistakenly believe they can help him/her to change

- They are not aware of the fact that they allow abuse to occur

The victim stays in the situation for a variety of reasons. The abuser may control the finances, the vehicle(s), or other assets, which limits the victim to what they can and cannot do (leaving them with little skills for employment, and such low self-esteem that they are often afraid to take the steps to improve their conditions. The victim also understands the possibility of being seriously harmed or even murdered if they attempt to leave.

The victim may believe having a child will "fix" things, so upon conceiving they are already placing a child, albeit a fetus, in a role no child should take: the protector of the adult. Yet abusers will beat a pregnant woman as often as a non-pregnant woman. Their abuse will eventually include the child.

Domestic abuse happens in every country, in every state, city, town, village, and neighborhood. It occurs among Jews, Muslims, Christians, Catholics, Buddhists, Atheists, and Agnostics – all of the religious persuasions and ethnicities that dot the world. All demographics are affected, social status, race, creed, or color of skin. Domestic abuse occurs in both heterosexual and homosexual relationships. Instances of it are found in the Bible, the Quran, and other sacred texts. It is a regrettable part of our society.

It is already difficult enough to know exactly how many women are in abusive relationships, but it is even more difficult to know how many men suffer abuse. Men have historically been less likely to report instances of abuse because they may see it as a negative toward their masculinity, and what a "real" man is supposed to be and do, and are often uninformed about resources that are available to them. In addition, homosexual men may be reluctant to report abuse, due to being afraid of having their sexual orientation exposed.

Far too many still do not understand how the varying forms of abuse are manifest, and may believe that incidents of sexual, emotional, financial, and religious abuse are not, in fact, abuse. Thus, when the victim is experiencing such types of abuse, they often discount it, and do not understand it for what it is, instead see interpreting the abusive behavior as a flawed character trait, or due to another stressor in the abuser's personality or life. The victim can also be re-victimized by authority figures who hold to such perspectives such as "it's not rape if you are married," or may be told fallacies by an abusive spouse such as "The Bible (or any religious text) says I own you, and you have to give it to me when I want."

Until the wheels are stopped, the abuse will continue perpetually.

# ADDITONAL RESOURCES

If you, or anyone you know, are a victim of domestic abuse, there is help available for you. Here are some resources that exist for the express purpose of helping you to lead the healthy and peaceful life you deserve.

The National Domestic Violence Hotline contact information:
www.thehotline.org
1-800-799-SAFE (7233)
1-800-787-3244 (TTY)

National Coalition Against Domestic Violence (NCADV)
www.ncadv.org
(303) 839-1852
mainoffice@ncadv.org

Information for men who are in a violent relationship:
www.helpguide.org/articles/abuse/help-for-abused-men.htm
Call 1-888-7HELPLINE (1-888-743-5754) US & Canada
Call 01823 334244 or 0808 801 0327 in the UK

To learn about bipolar disorder:
"Bipolar Disorder in Adults" (2012). National Institute of Mental Health, Department of Health & Human Services, publisher. NIH Publication 12-3679
Available as a free download at:
https://infocenter.nimh.nih.gov/pubstatic/TR%2015-3679/TR%2015-3679.pdf

# ACKNOWLEDGEMENTS

Many thanks to the following agencies, and individuals, all of which are in Tennessee unless otherwise specified:

- The Memphis Police Department and Ruth Murray, Central Records Division
- The Shelby County Criminal Clerk's Office, Chief Administrative Officer Danny W. Kail
- The Jackson Police Department and Ms. R. Crayton, Central Records Division
- The Hardin County Clerk's Office
- The Crump Police Department
- The Selmer Police Department
- The McNairy County Clerk's Office, and Mr. Byron Maxedon, Clerk
- The General Sessions of McNairy County Circuit Court
- The General Sessions Civil Division of Shelby County and B. Davis
- The Shelby County Sheriff's Office and D. L. Fessenden, Legal Advisor
- The Shelby County Office of the District Attorney
- The Tennessee Department of Corrections and the records management division
- The Florida Department of Corrections
- The Texas Department of Corrections
- The Federal Bureau of Prisons
- The Adamsville Police Department
- Mr. John Thomson, Director of the 25th Tennessee Western District Drug Task Force
- The Southaven Police Department and Lt. Little, Mississippi
- The Newspaper Archives Section of the beautiful Benjamin L. Hooks Memphis Central Library

As well as the hundreds of staff members, investigators, officers, agents, and people of government agencies in Tennessee, Texas, Florida, and Mississippi who assisted in researching, providing records, and patiently answering an author's many questions.

Special recognition to Marie Finney of the Memphis Criminal Court Clerk's Offices and her staff for outstanding service and excellent company. Marie, I still owe you lunch.

A huge "THANK YOU" to Shelby County Assistant District Attorney Pamela D. Fleming for taking the time to work with me, and for knowing where to find the best barbeque in Memphis.

Thank you to Walter Norris, Memphis Police Department Lieutenant (Retired). As an author, you appreciate the importance of obtaining facts. As an officer, you and your team did an outstanding job in the case. Thank you for your sincere concern for crime victims.

Thank you to the families and friends of Ejaz Ahmad for their honesty, and for trusting me with their story.

Thank you to Leah Ward and her family and friends for their honesty, and for trusting me with their story.

Thank you to everyone at Wild Blue Press for believing in this project. Big thanks to my amazing editor, Jacqueline Burch.

Special thanks to my family and friends for their support, love, and understanding that when I fall into a project and disappear, it does not mean I don't love them.

A special, special "Thank you" to Memphis, Tennessee, a city I love for endless hospitality, personality, adventure, and excellent food at any hour of the night.

And thank you, St. Michael, for covering me with wings when I need it ... and for letting me run with scissors because sometimes I need that, too.

May St. Michael enfold you all in his wings as well.

# ABOUT THE AUTHOR

Criminologist Judith A. Yates is an award-winning true crime author and the editor of *True Crime: Case Files Magazine*. She contributes to several online publications including the website *www.corrections.com* and *Serial Killer Quarterly*. Her collegiate work has appeared in national journals. Her nonfiction work has appeared in multiple media formats.

Ms. Yates has taught crime prevention and education for over twenty-five years and is an expert on domestic violence education and prevention. She holds a Master of Science in Criminal Justice; she was recognized for her thesis on school violence. She is currently completing her PhD in Criminal Justice. Ms. Yates has been employed in corrections, loss prevention, private investigations, and in criminal justice education. Ms. Yates has attended law enforcement schools & training across the country, to include Texas, New Mexico, Tennessee, and Maryland. She is a victim's advocate and supports law enforcement.

She performs guest speaker presentations and training across the country for various organizations, to include the Texas Association of Legal Investigators; National Parents, Families, & Friends of Lesbians & Gays (PFLAG), The International Association for Identification, The Federal Bureau of Prisons, and the Tennessee Correctional Association.

Ms. Yates shares her home in Kentucky with her family and rescued horses, dogs, cats, and snakes. Her hobbies include volunteering with animal rescue groups, playing video games, photography, and creating artwork using found objects. She has phobias of alligators, dental offices, and circus clowns, though not always in that order.

Please see www.truecrimebook.net for more information and for booking Ms. Yates for a book signing or speaking engagement.

# OTHER BOOKS BY JUDITH A. YATES

*The Devil You Know: The Crime They Said "Can't Happen Here"*

Winner of the 2014 Killer Nashville's Silver Falchion for True Crime

*How to Recognize the Devil: Common Sense Self-Defense & Crime Prevention Handbook*

"An excellent and important book that should really be required reading in America's high schools before ignorance and excuses for interpersonal violence and/or abuse are locked in ... I suggest buying this book as a gift ... it would truly be a gift of love, and perhaps even life."

- Burl Barer, Edgar Award Winner and bestselling author of true crime, mystery fiction, supernatural thrillers, and pop culture

*When Nashville Bled: The Untold Stories of Serial Killer Paul Dennis Reid*

"A well-written true story that captures a horrible time in the city ... the author tells the story of each person who was taken away by this monster. A sad, but factual, book told with compassion. A must-read for any true crime enthusiast. Highly recommended!"

- Dr. R.J. Parker, award-winning and best-selling true crime author, criminologist, and owner of R.J. Parker Publishing, Inc.

*An Elephant Snuffled My Tent: Finding Myself in the African Bush*

An autobiographical account, partnered with stunning photographs, on becoming whole again after the corporate world fragments your life.

Use this link to sign up for advance notice
of Judith A. Yates' Next Book:
http://wildbluepress.com/AdvanceNotice

Word-of-mouth is critical to an author's long-term success.
If you appreciated this book please leave a review on the
Amazon sales page:
http://wbp.bz/ sheisevilamazon

## Another Great True Crime Read
## From WildBlue Press

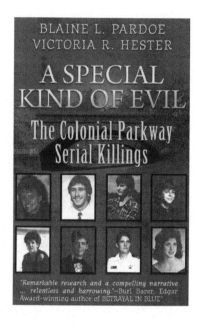

In the late 1980s, a predator stalked the Tidewater region of Virginia, savagely murdering his carefully selected his prey. He, or they, demonstrated a special kind of evil, and to this day have evaded justice. This is the first comprehensive look at the Colonial Parkway Murders and sheds new light on the victims, the crimes, and the investigation.

Read More: **http://wbp.bz/aspecialkindofmurder**

WILDBLUE
PRESS

**Available Now From WildBlue Press:**
**DADDY'S LITTLE SECRET by Denise Wallace**

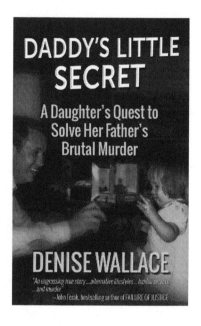

The poignant true crime story about a daughter who, upon her father's murder, learns of his secret double-life. She had looked the other way about other secrets of his, as well — deadly secrets that could help his killer escape the death penalty, should she come forward. An inside look at the complex and fascinating psyche of a father who shared an uncommon bond with his daughter.

Read More: **http://wbp.bz/dls**

## More True Crime You'll Love From WildBlue Press

**RAW DEAL** by Gil Valle

RAW DEAL: The Untold Story of the NYPD's "Cannibal Cop" is the memoir of Gil Valle, written with co-author Brian Whitney. It is part the controversial saga of a man who was imprisoned for "thought crimes," and a look into an online world of dark sexuality and violence that most people don't know exists, except maybe in their nightmares.

**wbp.bz/rawdeal**

**BETRAYAL IN BLUE** by Burl Barer & Frank C. Girardot Jr.
Adapted from Ken Eurell's shocking personal memoir, plus hundreds of hours of exclusive interviews with the major players, including former international drug lord, Adam Diaz, and Dori Eurell, revealing the truth behind what you won't see in the hit documentary THE SEVEN FIVE.

**wbp.bz/bib**

**THE POLITICS OF MURDER** by Margo Nash

*"A chilling story about corruption, political power and a stacked judicial system in Massachusetts."*–John Ferak, bestselling author of FAILURE OF JUSTICE.

**wbp.bz/pom**

**FAILURE OF JUSTICE** by John Ferak

If the dubious efforts of law enforcement that led to the case behind MAKING A MURDERER made you cringe, your skin will crawl at the injustice portrayed in FAILURE OF JUSTICE: A Brutal Murder, An Obsessed Cop, Six Wrongful Convictions. Award-winning journalist and bestselling author John Ferak pursued the story of the Beatrice 6 who were wrongfully accused of the brutal, ritualistic rape and murder of an elderly widow in Beatrice, Nebraska, and then railroaded by law enforcement into prison for a crime they did not commit.

**wbp.bz/foj**